Illustrator:
Keith Vasconcelles

Editor:
Stephanie Buehler, M.P.W., M.A.

Editorial Project Manager:
Ina Massler Levin, M.A.

Editor-in-Chief:
Sharon Coan, M.S. Ed.

Art Director:
Elayne Roberts

Cover Artist:
Sue Fullam

Product Manager:
Phil Garcia

Imaging:
Alfred Lau

Publishers:
Rachelle Cracchiolo, M.S. Ed.
Mary Dupuy Smith, M.S. Ed.

Whole Language Unit
for
FAVORITE TALES

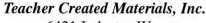

Authors:

Deborah Plona Cerbus, M.A.
and
Cheryl Feichtenbiner Rice, M.A.

Teacher Created Materials, Inc.
6421 Industry Way
Westminster, CA 92683
www.teachercreated.com

©1995 Teacher Created Materials, Inc.
Reprinted, 2004
Made in U.S.A.
ISBN-1-55734-204-0

Table of Contents

Introduction

The purpose of whole language is to provide a literacy-rich environment in which children learn to use and enjoy written and spoken language naturally. The children become immersed in print and use their developing language skills in purposeful activities. In Whole Language Units for Favorite Tales, children learn about classic children's literature. They will learn to enjoy and increase their proficiency in written and spoken language. With the teacher modeling oral language, the children will appreciate literature, hear rhyming patterns, and learn new concepts. Children will use thinking skills such as brainstorming and predicting, in addition to creating their own innovations.

Each unit in this book begins with a children's literature selection. Use your classroom, school, and public library as you gather literature for each unit. In addition, each unit contains some or all of the following:

- related literature
- sample lesson plans
- center ideas
- home/school connecting activities
- original poetry
- flannel-board patterns
- reproducible little books
- art projects

- songs
- games
- phonics activities
- recipes
- riddles
- retelling activities
- sequencing activities
- culminating activities

Activities may be chosen to fit the needs of your classroom and your teaching style. Although each unit is designed to last approximately one week, it may be lengthened or shortened to suit any curriculum.

What Is Whole Language?

Whole language programs are based on the belief that children should learn to read and write naturally, just as they learned to speak. The goals are for the children to learn to read and write and to learn to love reading and writing.

In a whole language program, skill development and enrichment activities are arranged around a literacy experience. Instead of teaching reading, language, writing, spelling, and speaking as separate units, the teacher relates all of these to a particular book, story, or poem. Students listen to whole text and experience its meaning. This is accomplished not just by asking a few questions about the story, but by immersing the class in repeated experiences with the story. Children learn best and become involved in their learning by listening, speaking, reading, writing, drawing, and touching. When possible, students should act out or "play" the stories.

Whole language strategies involve a series of daily activities based on books. The teacher reads aloud to the children several times a day for their enjoyment, modeling enthusiasm and good reading behavior. Listening together gives the children a common background to use in extending the literature throughout the school day.

Since literature is the focus of the whole language classroom, children are given plenty of opportunities to practice reading. Children listen to stories, rhymes, and poems and are encouraged to make predictions, inferences, and deductions. They are also given time to read independently. Reading is supported with activities that combine listening, writing, speaking, and illustrating.

Writing is also an essential component of a balanced whole language program. Children use ideas or patterns from stories they have read to create new stories. Younger children need lots of directions, modeling, and suggestions from the teacher. Students use invented spelling during creative writing. They are encouraged not to worry about correct spelling, but to sound out a word and spell it the best they can. Spelling correction may intimidate very young writers. Older students can correct and edit a second draft.

A whole language classroom provides a print-rich environment. Walls and bulletin boards are covered with labeled pictures and creative writing. New words from instructional units are displayed on experience charts or on word bank posters. Copies of literature and Big Books are available in a reading center along with books written by the students. The entire classroom has a colorful and stimulating environment with specific work centers, a variety of materials for reading and writing that are changed frequently, and numerous displays of students' work and projects.

Preparing for a Whole Language Unit

Before using a whole language unit, prepare the materials necessary for teaching the unit. Some general suggestions are given below.

Gathering Materials: Go to your school or public library to locate the featured literature which relates to the theme. Look up and locate the songs listed at the beginning of each unit. Check to see if the unit requires any props or puppets for storytelling or story keepsakes for the children to take home. Read the sample lesson plans to see if any other materials, such as sentence strips or chart paper, are required.

Sending Parent Letters: Each unit contains a parent letter. Copy it and send it home either before the unit begins or on the first day of the unit.

Using the Poetry: Make an overhead transparency of the poetry page. You might also want to print the poem on chart paper or on sentence strips. Individual copies of the poem can be kept in a poetry folder.

Making Little Books: Reproduce the pages of the little books. Books may be assembled before the lesson or students may help complete the following steps: 1) Cut on the dotted lines. 2) Check to make sure the pages are in the right order. 3) Staple the pages together. 4) Students may use crayons or markers to color their little books. 5) The books should be read together as a class; then, partners can take turns reading them to each other; and finally, students can take the books home to be shared with parents.

Using Activity Pages: Reproduce appropriate unit activity pages for the children. Directions for using the pages are given in the sample lesson plans for each unit.

Preparing the Games: Reproduce the game pieces on heavy paper. Color and laminate all the pieces and store them in self-sealing bags. Label each bag with the name of the game.

Using the Patterns: Patterns are provided with many of the units. Trace these patterns onto felt or Pellon® 930 for use on a flannel board. Some patterns may be enlarged, traced on tagboard, and laminated for use in various center activities or on bulletin boards. The patterns can also be used to make stick puppets or story props for retelling the stories.

Setting Up Classroom Centers

Many different types of centers are appropriate in a whole language classroom. The following are general suggestions for types of centers and the materials needed in them. Refer to the "Centers" page in each unit for specific center activities.

☆ **Reading Center:** Fiction and nonfiction books (including copies of featured literature), poetry books, magazines, Big Books, copies of little books, student-made books, word charts, a pocket chart, a flannel board, sentence strips, chart paper, overhead projector, comfortable chairs, pillows, and rugs.

☆ **Listening Center:** Tape recorder and headphones, copies and tapes of the little books and the featured literature selections.

☆ **Writing Center:** A variety of type of paper, pencils, washable markers, crayons, alphabet stamps, wooden letters, magnetic letters and board, word bank posters, pictionaries, typewriters, a computer with a simple word processing program, and blank journals and books.

☆ **Social Studies Center:** A globe, maps, pictures of people from around the world, an interest table for items from other countries, picture books and informational books about people and families around the world, career hats.

☆ **Math Center:** A flannel board, number stamps, wooden numbers, magnetic numbers and board, an estimating jar, pattern blocks, small cubes, tangrams, small objects for counting (such as plastic teddy bears), a floor graph, a balance scale.

☆ **Science Center:** Observation journals, poster and pictures, science books (both picture books and informational texts), a science "please touch" table, plants and seeds, seed and flower catalogs, science magazines such as *Ranger Rick* and *Your Big Backyard,* and a class pet.

☆ **Art Center:** White and colored paper of various sizes and textures, paints, crayons, markers, colored chalk, clay, glitter, tissue paper, old magazines, and fabric scraps and trims.

☆ **Dramatic Play Center:** Child-sized furniture, kitchen area, dishes and play food, a telephone, dress-up clothes, a dollhouse, muticultural dolls, puppets, and stuffed animals, blocks of all shapes and sizes (wooden, plastic, cardboard), plastic interconnecting blocks, vehicles signs, a barn with farm animals.

Sample Lesson Plans

Featured Literature: *The House That Jack Built*

Author: Elizabeth Falconer

Publisher: William Heinemann Ltd., London, 1990; Ideals Publishing Corporation, Nashville, Tennessee

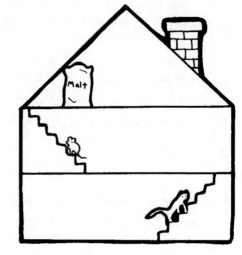

Summary: This beautifully illustrated book, first published in 1755, in both rhyme and rebus tells the chain of events that begins when Jack builds his house.

Additional Literature: *The House That Jack Built* illustrated by Emily Bolan (Dutton Children's Books, 1992); *The House That Jack Built* illustrated by Paul Galdone (McGraw-Hill, 1961); *The Farmer in the Dell* illustrated by Mary Maki Rae (Viking Penguin, 1988); *The Cake That Mack Ate* by Rose Robert (Atlantic Monthly Press, 1986); *The Napping House* by Audrey Wood (HBJ, 1984).

Related Songs: "The Farmer in the Dell," a traditional singing game, can be found in the book, *The Farmer in the Dell,* illustrated by Mary Maki Rae (Viking Penguin, 1988).

Day 1: Before reading *The House That Jack Built*, explain to your students that while this rhyme has been in print for over two hundred years, it originally was a story passed orally from parent to child. Preview the rhyme with your class by looking at the book's illustrations and borders. Point out that because the rhyme is very old, some of its words differ from words that are used today, then explain the following words: rebus, malt (grain that has been allowed to sprout before being used; you may wish to make Malt-o-Meal for students to sample), crumpled, maiden, forlorn, tattered, priest, shorn, cock, sowing. Then model the first oral reading for your class, encouraging students to "read along" by looking at the rebus pictures. Reread the book, encouraging children to join in on the rhyming words.

You should also make flannel board shapes using the patterns on pages 18 - 20 for use in retelling the story. Keep the shapes with your flannel board at the Reading Center for children to use independently.

This rhyme perfectly lends itself to sequencing activities. Write the lines of the rhyme on sentence strips for sequencing correctly in your pocket chart. The pictures on page 22 can be cut apart, enlarged on a copier machine, and used to make a graphic card for each line of the rhyme. Read the lines from the sentence strips and match them to the corresponding picture card. Later, keep the strips and cards at your Reading Center for children to use on their own.

In your reading area, make a bulletin board displaying "The House That Jack Built Quilt." Use pastel colors of construction paper cut into 9" (23 cm) squares and print one line from the rhyme across the bottom of each. Put your students in pairs, then assign each pair a line to illustrate. Remind the students that each square is important, as the quilt will not make sense without all the lines. Attach each illustrated square to your bulletin board in the correct sequence. Then run white rick-rack trim between the squares and as a border around the entire quilt.

Send home the Parent Letter on page 10.

Sample Lesson Plans *(cont.)*

Day 2: Begin today's activities by working with your students to retell the rhyme using "The House That Jack Built Quilt."

Next, read another version of the rhyme. The Bolan version, with its bold setting and palm trees, provides a good contrast to the English countryside in the Falconer version. Using the picture cards from your pocket chart, choose a different student to hold each one. Instruct the students to stand and display their card when they hear the corresponding line of the rhyme.

After this matching activity, encourage your students to compare and contrast the two versions using questions such as, are the same lines used in each? Are the same characters and props used? How are the two books different? How are they the same?

Find settings from both versions on a globe, then discuss how different places on the earth have different climates. Talk about how climate affects the types of plants and animals found in a region, as well as the types of shelter and clothing used by its human inhabitants.

Prepare a strip of adding machine tape with the word chunk "-at" at the top to use for making a word family list. Tell students that they will be helping you search the text for words that rhyme with "cat" and "rat." Explain to your students that both these words use the "-at" word chunk and that more words may be made by adding different letters as beginning sounds. Go through the text with the students and record other similar rhyming words on the prepared strip. Encourage children to think of more words that use the same "-at" chunk (fat, hat, sat, etc.). The text can also be used to find words that use the "-orn" word chunk for another word family list. Reproduce these lists so that children may practice them. Post the list at your Reading Center, making additional word family lists for other word chunks during the year.

Reproduce "The House That Jack Built" rhyme on a large sheet of chart paper or on an overhead transparency and practice reading it with the children. Then have the children color, cut, and assemble their own little books of the rhyme to take home (see pages 12 - 17).

Day 3: Begin today by again using "The House That Jack Built Quilt" to retell the rhyme. This time, you may wish to have individual students do the retelling.

Read another version of the cumulative rhyme, such as the one by Jenny Stow that is set in the Carribbean. (If you have access to *Reading Rainbow* on video cassette, this book is a featured selection.) Guide your students to compare and contrast the text, illustrations, and setting from this book with the others you have read. Find this new setting on the globe and extend your students' geographic awareness by pointing out that the plants, the clothing, and the house shown in the book relate to the climate of the Caribbean.

Use the sentence strips from your pocket chart to read the rhyme together. Then switch two of the sentence strips and challenge your students to switch them back to the correct sequence. Repeat, switching two or more strips. As you read along with your students, help them attend to individual words as well as sequencing skills.

Reproduce pages 21 and 22 for children to create a Story Retelling House by having them color, cut, and glue pictures from page 22 onto the house shape on page 21.

Sample Lesson Plans *(cont.)*

Day 4: Retell the cumulative rhyme using the sentence strips. Invite one child to come up and switch two of the sentence strips and another child to switch them back in the correct sequence. This activity can be done later by children in pairs at the Reading Center.

Read another version of the rhyme today, such as the Galdone book. Compare the text, illustrations, and setting with previously read versions.

Reproduce and use the riddles on page 23 with the children to review their knowledge about the characters in the rhyme.

Extend your students' learning by introducing Learning Centers for this theme. See page 9 for ideas.

Day 5: As your concluding project for this week's theme, create a house in your classroom. Use a large appliance cardboard box covered with colored butcher paper. Let the children decorate the box with construction paper doors, windows, curtains, chimney, bushes, mailbox, etc. Make a large banner for the house such as, "This is the house that Room 3 built." Take photographs of the house as it is being built and later display the pictures with suitable captions, for example, "This is Christina who made the curtains/That hang in the house that Room 3 Built." Your classroom house could be used all year for various learning centers.

Read your class' favorite version of *The House That Jack Built* and again have individual students stand up with a matching picture card at the appropriate time. Then introduce the traditional singing game, "The Farmer in the Dell." Have your students make a circle and choose a child to be the "farmer," who will go to the center of the circle and choose a "wife," etc. Encourage your students to compare and contrast the cumulative rhyme with the cumulative song.

Extend your students' experience with cumulative tales by reading *The Napping House* by Audrey Wood and *The Cake That Mack Ate* by Rose Robart, encouraging children to notice the similarities to *The House That Jack Built.*

8

Sample Centers

Reading Centers: At this center, keep copies of all the different versions of *The House That Jack Built* for children to read independently. Make several extra copies of "The House That Jack Built" little book for children to read independently or in small groups. A copy of the Story Retelling House, "The House That Jack Built Quilt," and the flannel board shapes may be placed here as retelling aids.

Children also may use the sentence strips and picture cards introduced on Day 1 to practice sequencing the lines of the rhyme. Keep your word family list of "-at" words posted here, and encourage children to listen to each other as they read.

Writing Center: Children may draw pictures of their own houses and then complete a sentence frame to identify their houses and practice their addresses such as "My name is _____. I live at _____."

Math Center: Put several small plastic houses, similar to those found in a popular board game, in the center's Estimating Jar. Put ten houses into an identical jar to give your students a reference for their estimates and discuss with your students whether their estimates will be less than ten, more than ten, or equal to ten. If you use houses of two different colors, children also may guess whether there are more houses of Color "A" or Color "B" in the Estimating Jar.

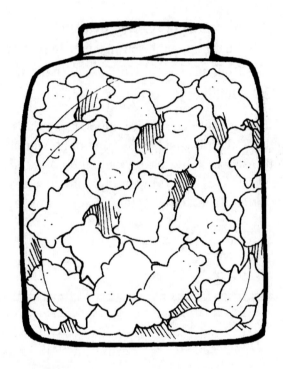

If you have the Falconer version of *The House That Jack Built*, children may count and tally the number of animals in each of the decorative borders. You may wish to prepare a rebus-style chart to compile the tallied information.

Social Studies Center: Have a globe and world map available for children to locate the geographic regions illustrated in the different versions of *The House That Jack Built*. Have available non-fiction books such as *Houses and Homes* by Ann Morris so students may learn about housing around the world.

Block Center: Provide a variety of wood building blocks and plastic interconnecting blocks for the children to use in building their own houses. When "builders" complete their houses, have them write a sentence such as "This is the house that Jenna built" on a large index card folded in half. Display the houses with their cards on a table set aside for this purpose.

Art Center: Discuss the illustration styles in the different versions of *The House That Jack Built*. Explain that tempera colors produce pictures that are bright and bold, while watercolors are softer. Tell students at this center to choose their favorite medium to paint houses. Have them add details to their paintings to show the geographic setting of the house (trees, plants, people, animals, etc.).

Parent Letter

Dear Parents,

We are currently working on a unit based upon the classic cumulative rhyme "The House That Jack Built." We will be using this rhyme to practice our sequencing and retelling skills. We also will read several versions of the rhyme and complete a variety of activities in reading, writing, math, social studies, and music. Each of the children will be making a little booklet of "The House That Jack Built" that will be brought home to share with you.

Please encourage your child to tell you what was learned at school each day to reinforce learning. Other activities we have planned include:

1. Making a Story Retelling House.
2. Learning about settings in different parts of the world.
3. Making a list of words that rhyme with "at".
4. Building our own classroom house.

Since this unit deals with houses, it provides us with an opportunity for the children to practice their own addresses and phone numbers. Please write the correct information on the house shape below, have your child color the house, and proudly display it on your refrigerator. Listen to your child practice saying this until it is memorized. These are important facts for all young children to learn. Your help is greatly appreciated!

Sincerely,

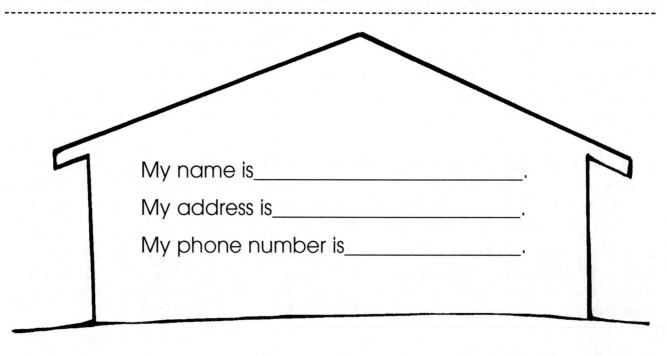

My name is_____.

My address is_____.

My phone number is_____.

The House That Jack Built

This is the farmer sowing his corn

That kept the cock that crowed in the morn

 That woke the priest all shaven and shorn

That married the man all tattered and torn

That kissed the maiden all forlorn

That milked the cow with the crumpled horn

That tossed the dog

 That worried the cat

That chased the rat

That ate the malt

That lay in the house

That Jack built.

Making Little Books

My Little Book of
The House That Jack Built

Name_____

This is the farmer sowing his corn

1

Making Little Books *(cont.)*

That kept the cock that crowed in the morn   2

That woke the priest all shaven and shorn   3

Making Little Books *(cont.)*

- -

That married the man all tattered and torn   4

- -

That kissed the maiden all forlorn   5

- -

Making Little Books *(cont.)*

That milked the cow with the crumpled horn   **6**

That tossed the dog   **7**

Making Little Books *(cont.)*

That worried the cat   **8**

That chased the rat   **9**

Making Little Books *(cont.)*

That ate the malt

10

That lay in the house
That Jack built.

11

Patterns

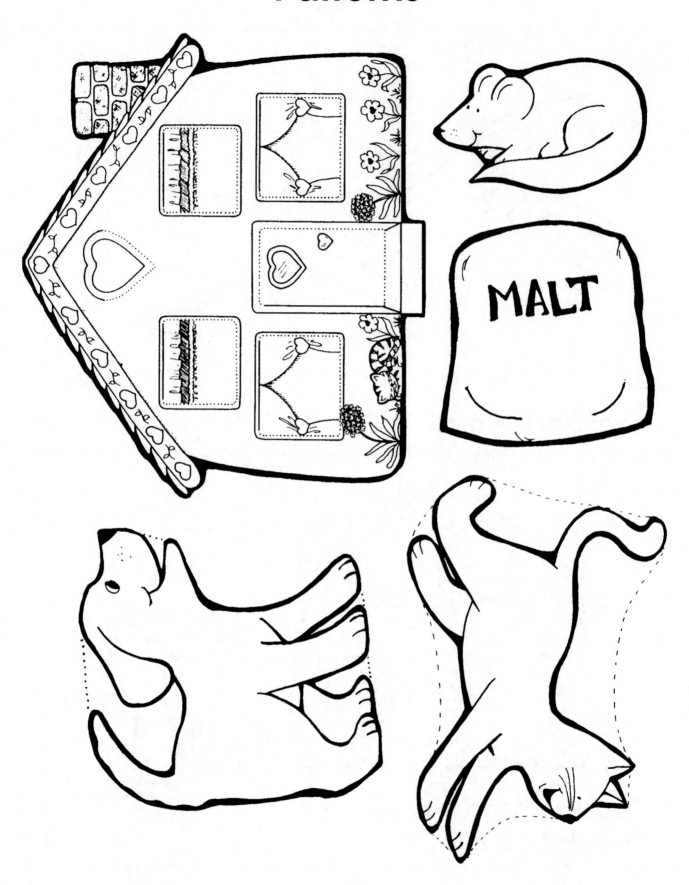

MALT

18

Patterns *(cont.)*

Patterns *(cont.)*

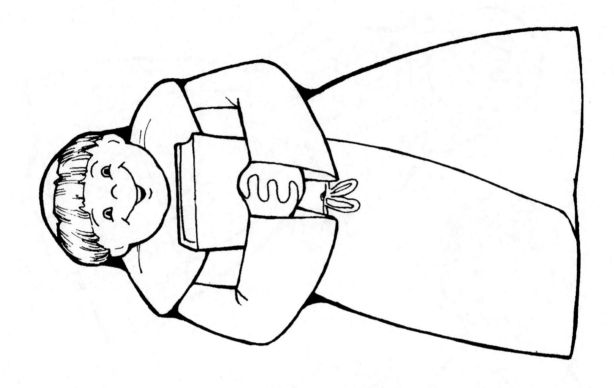

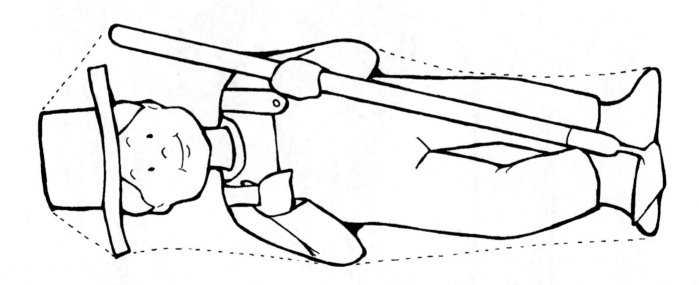

Name _____

Story Retelling House
The House That Jack Built

See directions on page 7.

Story Retelling House *(cont.)*

Directions: Color these pictures. Cut out the boxes. Glue them in the correct sequence on the Story Retelling House on page 21.

1 house	2 malt	3 rat	4 cat
5 dog	6 cow	7 maiden	8 man
9 priest	10 cock	11 farmer	

The House That Jack Built Riddles

I'm where you live, a
  place to play,
A place for fun all through
  the day.
What am I?

I'm a cereal grain,
  nice and sweet,
Eaten with milk, I can't
  be beat.
What am I?

I am small and come out at night.
I may give you quite a fright.
What am I?

I chased the rat.
Imagine that!
What am I?

I like to run at the park.
Big or small – I can bark.
What am I?

On a farm, I do live.
Lots of milk, I will give.
What am I?

     #204 Whole Language Units for Favorite Tales

Sample Lesson Plans

Featured Literature: *The Three Bears*

Author: Byron Barton

Publisher: HarperCollins Publishers, 1991

Summary: There are many versions of this classic tale about the three bears and their unexpected guest, Goldilocks. Byron Barton's bright, colorful illustrations and simple text make this selection a perfect choice for young readers.

Additional Literature: *Goldilocks and The Three Bears* by James Marshall (Dial Books, 1988); *Goldilocks* by Dom De Luise (Simon & Shuster, 1992); *Goldilocks and The Three Bears* by Armand Eisen (Alfred A. Knopf, 1989); *When Goldilocks Went To The House Of The Bears* by Jenny Rendall (Scholastic, 1986); *Alaska's Three Bears* by Shannon Cartwright (Paws IV Publishing Co., Box 2364 Homer, Alaska 99603); *Somebody and the Three Blairs* by Marilyn Tolhurst (Orchard Books, 1990); *Goldilocks and the Three Bears* by Jan Brett (Dodd, Mead, & Company, 1987); *The Three Bears* by Paul Galdone (Clarion Books, 1972); *Bear In Mind - A Book of Bear Poems* selected by Bobbye S. Goldstein (Puffin Books, 1989).

Related Songs: "Bear Song" by Marie Wheeler; "Time For Sleeping" by Terri Crosbie; "Little Bear" by Carla C. Skjong; "Are You Sleepy?" by Sue Brown; *Animal Piggyback Songs* (Warren Publishing House, 1990).

Day 1: Start this "beary" special unit by finding out what the children know about real bears. Make a K-W-L chart by listing what the children *know* and what they *want* to know about bears. Later in the week, complete the chart by adding what the children have *learned*. You may also wish to cut out large bear shapes (see pattern on p. 35) from tagboard to laminate for recording bear facts and questions that the group has brainstormed with you.

For today's read aloud, use the Barton version of *The Three Bears*. To create interest prior to reading the story, tuck the book and some props such as toy bears and bowls into a picnic basket. Show the basket to the children and have them guess what story will be read as the items are revealed one by one. When they guess the title, discuss Goldilocks' name and why that name is a good choice for her. Ask the children if they can think of other appropriate names for the mischievous girl.

Read the story aloud, encouraging the children to join in on the familiar phrases such as "just right." Discuss the behavior of the storybook bears, comparing it to what the children know about real bears. Decide whether the story is real or fantasy and have students state their reasons as to why this is a fantasy selection.

Display "The Three Bears" poem from page 30 on a large piece of chart paper or on an overhead transparency. Underline or write the word "three" in a different color to draw attention to it. Encourage the children to identify other words which occur frequently in the poem such as "bear."

Send home the Parent Letter on page 29.

Sample Lesson Plans *(cont.)*

Day 2: Begin by reviewing yesterday's poem, then read related poems from *Bear in Mind—A Book of Bear Poems.* Write some of these poems on chart paper that has been cut into bear shapes or on overhead transparencies for later use in the Reading Center.

Read *When Goldilocks Went To The House Of The Bears*, available in big book format. Before you begin, talk about the unusual title and discuss the humorous illustration on the cover. Have the children predict how this story might be the same or different from Barton's version. While reading, call attention to the rhyme and pattern found in the story. Afterwards, make a list of elements common to both versions.

Finally, have the children work in small groups to create story maps by drawing the important events of the story in order. Have each group present their story map to practice retelling and sequencing skills.

Day 3: Introduce other versions of *The Three Bears* such as the classics by Brett or Galdone or humorous versions by Marshall or De Luise. This latter story is rather unusual as it has an Italian flavor, with Goldilocks eating *pasta e fagioli* (macaroni and bean soup) and joining the bears for lunch. Recipes are included in the back of the book for the soup as well as porridge and corn muffins.

Whatever versions are read, take time to compare and contrast the plot lines, text, illustrations, and endings of the stories. Be sure to talk about the styles of the bears' cottages as the children will be creating cottages later in the week.

Have each child color, cut and assemble a little book of the poem introduced on Day 1 (pages 31 to 34). Children should practice reading the book many times in class, then take the books home to share with their families.

Make a picture graph to find out which version of *The Three Bears* is the class favorite. List the titles or use copies of the cover of each book across a large sheet of bulletin board paper. Provide each child with a small bear shape on which to write their name. Each bear represents a vote. Let children place their bears in rows under their favorite version to create the graph. Count to see which book received the most and which the least votes. Ask the children to tell the reasons why they chose a certain book, for example, because they liked the style of illustration or the ending.

Sample Lesson Plans *(cont.)*

Day 4: Reread the class' favorite version of *The Three Bears*. Discuss how the story might be written if it featured three different animals or characters as preparation for children to work on their own story twists in the Writing Center.

Read *Somebody and the Three Blairs*, an interesting twist on the original folktale. In this story, a baby bear takes on the role of Goldilocks and is an unexpected visitor at the home of Mr. Blair, Mrs. Blair, and Baby Blair. Compare this version to the classic tale.

Practice reading the little books either as a group or as partner reading. Reread some of the bear poems introduced during the week and find out how many times the class can find the word "bear".

Treat the class to some porridge using your favorite recipe or the one found in the De Luise book. (Many flavored oatmeals are available at grocery stores and may be substituted for porridge.) After tasting the porridge, brainstorm and record a list of other breakfast foods on a large piece of chart paper. Reproduce copies of the list for the Reading or Writing Center where the children may illustrate the page. For now, give each child a 9" by 12" (23 cm x 30 cm) piece of construction paper and have them glue a real paper plate in the middle. Using crayons or markers, have the children draw their favorite breakfast foods on the plate or cut pictures of breakfast foods from magazines to glue on the plate. An adult may glue plastic utensils and a paper napkin next to the plate with a hot glue gun.

Extend the literature by inviting the class to join Learning Center activities related to the theme. See page 27 for some ideas.

Day 5: A performance of *Goldilocks and the Three Bears* is a perfect way to culminate this week of activities. Prior to the performance, reproduce the masks found on pages 37 - 40 on sturdy paper for children to color and cut out. Have them use the masks to practice retelling the story at the Reading Center. Assign the parts of Goldilocks, the bears, and two storytellers, and have the rest of the class form a bear "chorus". The bear chorus may be highlighted by having groups of four to five students take the stage to perform bear songs or poems before the play is acted. Give your production a catchy title such as "Goldilocks - The Musical". Decorate your staging area with a painted mural of the main characters as a backdrop. Add some decorated boxes or plastic milk crates stacked to different heights and place a variety of teddy bears on the containers. Invite other classes or the children's parents to a performance. You may want to serve a special treat, such as bear shaped cookies baked ahead of time.

Sample Centers

Reading Center: Create a cozy "cave" or "cottage" in this area by covering a large box with paper and having the class decorate it appropriately. Have available as many versions of *Goldilocks and the Three Bears* as you can find, including multiple copies of the Barton book for partner reading. Put bear poems from *Bear in Mind - A Book of Bear Poems* on sentence strips so that the children may reread them as they put the words in the pocket chart. If you have a bulletin board near this center, display some of the bear poems used in this unit for reading practice. Include the children's drawings or paintings of bears and a caption such as "Beary Good Poetry." You should also leave copies of the masks here as described on Day 5 so that children may retell and act out the story.

Writing Center: Invite the children to create their own twists of this favorite tale. For example, one child may write a story entitled, "Christopher and the Three Dogs". Model this activity by writing a group story before children use the center. Provide a variety of small stapled books and some pictures or books about animals to assist the children in their writing. The children can write their stories using invented spelling or dictate the story to an adult. After reading the finished stories to the class, put them on display.

Math Center: Set out an Estimating Jar containing small teddy shaped cookies or plastic bear counters, which can be found in an assortment of three sizes. Place teddy cookies or bear counters in an identical jar to use as a reference and ask students if their estimates should be more, less, or equal to ten. Students may also try to guess which size of bears are most prevalent in the assortment—small, medium, or large. Have the children record their estimates on a paper bear shape and then count the bears by tens to check their guesses.

To reinforce the concept of size, put out small, medium, and large beads and laces for stringing. Encourage the children to create patterns using the three sizes. You may provide bead cards if you would like the children to copy and extend patterns before creating their own.

For extra practice in counting skills, put out many stuffed bears and pictures of bears in your classroom. Have the children go on a "count the bears hunt" to total the number of bears found. Make copies of the bear shape found on page 35 and laminate them. Children may write their totals on the bear shape with a wipe-off pen. Teddy bears can also be used for sorting and classifying games. Challenge the children to group the bears by different characteristics, such as size and color.

Sample Centers *(cont.)*

Art Center: Encourage the children to look at the many styles of cottages found in the literature used throughout the week, then create a village of brightly painted cottages for your classroom. Make copies of the cottage shape found on page 36 for children to decorate in their own unique way with crayons or markers. The cottage pictures may be assembled into a class book called "Our Classy Cottages." Each child can dictate or write a sentence about why their cottage is special.

Duplicate one bear shape on page 35 on tagboard for each student. Cut out the bears and punch holes along the edge to create a lacing card. Provide thick yarn or long shoelaces for the children to string through the holes. After the cards are laced, tie off both loose ends on the back of the cards and have the children finish the bears by adding a face. They may cut the faces out of construction paper scraps or other materials such as buttons and small beads for more of a collage. For extra tying practice, provide ribbons, yarn, or narrow trim to create a bow for the bear's head or neck.

If you are planning a performance of *The Three Bears*, the children at this center could work on a mural for the scenery. Provide a long sheet of paper and have children paint a background on which they may glue paper figures that they have created from the story.

Science Center: Stock this center with non-fiction books and magazine articles about bears. Have the children work in teams of four to five students to look up information on specific bears. They should try to find out what the bear eats, where it lives, and any special habits or characteristics it has. Have each group complete a large mural to show the bear in its habitat. The background could be painted first, with bears and other details cut from construction paper and glued to the mural.

Block Center: Provide a variety of wood building blocks and plastic interconnecting blocks for the children to use in creating houses and cottages for the three bears. You may want to cut out pictures of houses from magazines or take photographs of the architecture common in your area for the children to study as they design their own buildings. Put some stuffed bears of all different sizes in this center and challenge the children to build houses to fit the various bears.

Dramatic Play Center: Set up the play house area as if it were Goldilocks' cottage. Include an apron and a bow for Goldilocks and props such as the three bowls, a pot for cooking porridge, three chairs, and three blankets in three sizes to represent the beds.

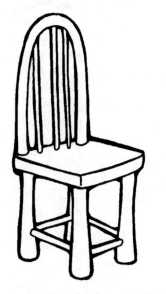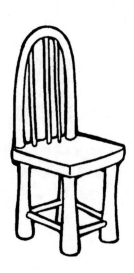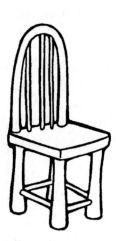

Parent Letter

Dear Parents,

Our new literature unit is *The Three Bears.* Our featured book will be *The Three Bears* by Byron Barton. This book has simple words and very colorful pictures, making it an ideal version for young children.

Some of the other stories we will read include traditional retellings such as *The Three Bears* by Paul Galdone and some humorous new books such as *Goldilocks and the Three Bears* by James Marshall. We will be comparing these books to find out what is the same or different about them.

From our readings we will choose a class favorite. We will participate in many activities to extend literature across the curriculum into areas such as math, art, science, and writing.

Your child will be bringing home a little book of a poem about the three bears to share with you. Some of our other activities will include the following:

1. Making a story map of the important events in the story.
2. Learning about real bears at the classroom Science Center.
3. Discussing the concept of small, medium and large as we classify objects by size.

Reading to your child is one of the most important activities you can do as a parent. Please use the bookmark below as you read some of your favorite tales together.

Sincerely,

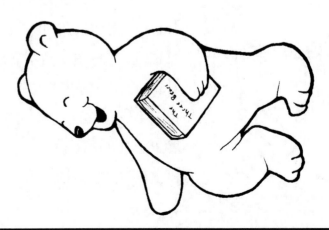

The Three Bears

Three furry bears
A nice family.
Papa and Mama
And baby makes three.
Three furry bears
Went for a walk.
Look out bears,
Here comes Goldilocks!
Three breakfast bowls
Filled with porridge sweet.
Goldilocks is hungry
For something good to eat.
Three nice chairs
A place to sit down.
Goldilocks broke the little one
And fell on the ground.
Three cozy beds
Big, medium, and small.
Goldilocks found baby's bed
Was the best one of all.
Three furry bears
Open the door.
The porridge is all gone,
The chair's on the floor.
Three furry bears
Find Goldilocks at last.
Run, run, run
Run home fast!

Making Little Books

- -

My Little Book of
The Three Bears

Name _____

- -

Three furry bears
A nice family.
Papa and Mama
And Baby makes three.

1

- -

Making Little Books *(cont.)*

**Three furry bears
Went for a walk.
Look out bears,
Here comes Goldilocks!**   **2**

**Three breakfast bowls
Filled with porridge sweet.
Goldilocks is hungry
For something good to eat.**   **3**

Making Little Books *(cont.)*

Three nice chairs

A place to sit down.

Goldilocks broke the little one

And fell on the ground.   **4**

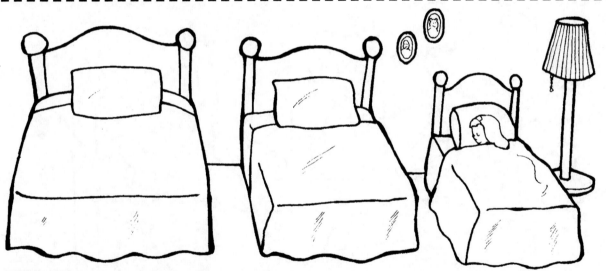

Three cozy beds

Big, medium, and small.

Goldilocks found baby's bed

Was the best one of all.   **5**

Making Little Books *(cont.)*

Three furry bears
Open the door.
The porridge is all gone
The chair's on the floor.

6

Three furry bears
Find Goldilocks at last.
Run, run, run
Run home fast.

7

Bear Pattern

Name _____

Cozy Cottage

Directions: Decorate this cottage to make it special for the three bears.

Story Masks

Directions: Color and cut out the masks. Staple them to wooden sticks and use them for retelling the story.

Papa

Story Masks *(cont.)*

Mama

Story Masks *(cont.)*

Baby

Story Masks *(cont.)*

Goldilocks

Sample Lesson Plans

Featured Literature: *The Three Little Pigs*

Author: Paul Galdone

Publisher: Scholastic, 1970

Summary: This is the classic tale of the three little pigs who set out on their own to build their own houses and make their way in the world, but find that the big bad wolf has other plans for them.

Additional Literature: *Three Little Pigs and the Big Bad Wolf* by Glen Rounds (Holiday House, 1992); *The Three Little Pigs* by Margot Zemach (Farrar, Straus and Giroux, 1988); *The Three Little Pigs* by Carla Dijs (Dell Publishing, 1991); *The Three Little Pigs* by James Marshall (Viking Penguin, 1989); *The Three Little Wolves and the Big Bad Pig* by Eugene Trivizas (Heinemann Young Books, 1993); *The Three Little Pigs* (Teacher Created Materials #551, 1992); *Building a House* by Byron Barton (Puffin, 1981); *Houses and Homes* by Ann Morris (Lothrop, Lee & Shepard, 1992); *The Fourth Little Pig* by Teresa Celsi (Steck-Vaughn, 1990); *The Three Little Javelinas* by Susan Lowell (Northland Pub., Co., 1992); *The True Story of the Three Little Pigs* by John Scieszka (Penguin Books, 1990).

Related Songs: "He'll Be Blowin' Down the Houses," *The Three Little Pigs* (Teacher Created Materials, 1992); "Who's Afraid of the Big Bad Wolf?" by Frank Churchill (The New Illustrated Disney Songbook, 1986).

Day 1: Introduce the tale of the three little pigs by showing your students a basket of straw, a basket of sticks, and a basket of bricks. Invite the children to identify which story they know that uses all three building materials. After they guess the story, encourage the children to tell the story as they know it, as many children will be eager to share their prior experience. Explain that there are many different versions of *The Three Little Pigs*, then invite them to be good listeners and enjoy the Galdone version. As you read, encourage the children to join in on the repetitive phrases such as "Not by the hair of my chinny chin chin."

Make sentence strips of lines such as these for your pocket chart for children to practice reading. When they are familiar with them, switch the strips and ask children to switch them back in the correct order. Make cards for the individual words in the sentence strips for children to match with words in the strips. Sentence strips and corresponding word cards then may be placed at your Reading Center for children to use independently.

Send home the Parent Letter on page 45.

Sample Lesson Plans *(cont.)*

Day 2: To develop comprehension skills, begin today by asking one of your students to retell the story of *The Three Little Pigs,* giving prompts as needed.

Then read another version of the story. The Zemach version or the Teacher Created Materials version of *The Three Little Pigs* would be good choices. The Teacher Created Materials version includes a big book, sentence strips, word cards, and a reproducible little book of the story which you may duplicate for each of your students.

Begin a Comparison Chart to record how the various versions are alike and different. To make a colorful chart, put a color copy of the cover of each book at the top of a large strip of bulletin board paper. List items to compare and contrast along the left side of the paper, including questions such as how many little pigs are in each story? How many wolves? What were the houses made of? What happened to the big, bad character?

Next, reproduce "The Three Little Pigs Chant" from page 46 on a large sheet of chart paper or on an overhead transparency. You can begin reading the chant aloud, alternating lines with your students. Reproduce copies of the little book for children to color, cut and assemble (pages 47 - 50). Have them practice the chant many times before students take the books home to share with their parents.

Day 3: Today ask a different child to retell the classic tale before you read yet more versions of *The Three Little Pigs* to your class.

Today would be a good day to read the Marshall version, the Rounds version, and the Dijs version. The Dijs "pop-up" version is unique, because the wolf does not eat the little pigs, nor does the wolf get eaten at the end. Add information from these versions to the Comparison Chart you began yesterday.

Encourage the children to identify the three materials which were used to build the houses in the story. Then create three large houses of your own to aid in retelling the story. Cut a large house shape from three 24" x 28" (61cm x 71cm) sheets of brown tagboard. Glue real straw to the first house and real sticks to the second house. For the third house, tear orange construction paper into pieces resembling bricks and glue them to the third shape. Attach a black tagboard roof to each and add details such as a door and windows. Use sentence strips to identify each type of house. The houses will make an attractive bulletin board for your Reading Center.

Discuss with your students what materials they discovered were used to build their homes as instructed in the activity sent home in the Parent Letter on Day 1. Use this information to make a graph. On a large sheet of bulletin board paper, glue the returned houses next to the appropriate label of "brick," "stucco," "wood," etc. Compare which materials are used most and which are used least.

Finally, read a non-fiction book such as *Building a House* by Byron Barton to your class. Invite a builder to visit your class to explain how houses are built in your area and to display materials and tools that are used. Have students assemble a second little book, this one on building houses, by reproducing pages 55 to 56.

Sample Lesson Plans *(cont.)*

Day 3, cont.:

To further extend your students' global awareness, read a book such as *Houses and Homes* by Ann Morris that shows the wide variety of houses found around the world. Use a globe or world map to locate some of the countries identified in the book. Discuss with your students why certain types of houses are appropriate in certain areas of the world.

Day 4: Have another of your students retell the traditional story of The Three Little Pigs. Explain that today you will be reading a slightly different version of the tale, told from the viewpoint of the wolf. Show the children *The True Story of the Three Little Pigs*, pointing out that the author is listed as "A. Wolf" as told to John Scieszka, and discuss point-of-view. When you finish, add information about this version to your Comparison Chart.

Discuss whether the pigs and wolf in the books read thus far are real or fantasy characters and ask students to explain their answers. Lead the children into a discussion of real animal homes. Share a collection of posters, books, and magazine pictures showing real animal homes and then put them in your Science Center.

To encourage more oral retelling, reproduce the stick puppet patterns on page 54 on tagboard for your students to make their own sets to practice dramatizing the story at the bulletin board display of the three houses.

Extend your student's learning by introducing the Learning Centers for this theme on page 44 .

Day 5: As your concluding activity for *The Three Little Pigs* unit, have your students work in groups of four or five (three pigs, a wolf, and possibly a narrator) to dramatize the story. Give your students ample time to practice their dramatizations, and invite another classroom in as an audience.

As another part of today's activities, make a graph to find out the class' favorite version of *The Three Little Pigs*. Give each child a sticker dot to place in a column under their favorite title. Reread this version to the class.

Explain that many favorite tales and rhymes use the number three. Have your students brainstorm a list of stories and rhymes which have this number in the title. Add to the list during the year and see how long it becomes.

Finally, share a very unusual version called *The Three Little Wolves and the Big Bad Pig* by Eugene Trivizas with your class. Versions such as *The Fourth Little Pig* and *The Three Little Javalinas* would be fun to share, too. Challenge your students to compare and contrast this humorous version with the traditional tale. Encourage them to think of unique titles for similar tales. Children could then dictate a similar story for you to record on chart paper or on an overhead transparency. Have students illustrate their unique new tale.

Sample Centers

Reading Center: Keep copies of all versions of *The Three Little Pigs* at this center.   Sentence strips and word cards introduced on Day 1 should be at this center with your pocket chart for independent practice. Keep an extra set of stick puppets and the flannel board shapes here for retelling the story. Make extra copies of the "Three Little Pigs" chant and the little books for use at this center.

Reproduce page 58 for students to make their own story map of *The Three Little Pigs.*

Writing Center: Children may choose to write a letter to the three little pigs or the wolf. If children write to the pigs, they could warn them of the dangers of houses made of unsafe materials. If they write to the wolf, they could point out more positive things that a wolf could spend his time doing besides bothering the pigs.

Math Center: Put some bolts or nails into your Estimating Jar. Put ten bolts or nails into an identical jar to use as a reference. Compare the amount of bolts or nails in the two jars and discuss whether the students' estimates should be more than, less than, or equal to ten.

For practice in comparing weights of objects, have several items available such as bolts, real sticks, real straw, wooden cubes, etc. Children can use a balance scale to weigh three items and compare the result to the weight of three different items.

Science Center: Display non-fiction books, magazine articles and posters about pigs, wolves, and animal homes at this center to encourage independent study. Duplicate page 57 for students to use in matching animals with their homes.

Social Studies Center: Keep several copies of *Building a House* by Byron Barton at this center. Books about houses around the world such as *House and Homes* by Ann Morris also could be kept here. Encourage students to use the classroom globe for locating where various types of houses may be found.

Dramatic Play Center: Children can use a variety of wood building blocks, plastic interconnecting blocks, straw, sticks, or cardboard to build their own houses. Have a "huffing and puffing contest" to see which houses can be blown down and which are sturdy enough to stand.

Art Center: Children can work at the art easel to paint "Pig Portraits," showing all three little pigs in a "family-portrait style" similar to the cover of the Galdone version of the tale.

Parent Letter

Dear Parents,

Our class is working on a new literature unit based upon the tale of *The Three Little Pigs.* We will be reading several versions of this classic story to compare and contrast. We will also be learning about real animal homes and finding out how homes are built for people.

During this unit, we will be completing activities across the curriculum, including:

1. Making a bulletin board display of three large houses, one of straw—one of sticks, and one of paper bricks.
2. Making stick puppets of the characters for retelling the story.
3. Creating a graph to show the materials used to build our own houses.

We need your help to complete our class graph about the materials used in building a house. Please take a tour of your house with your child to determine what building material (wood, brick, etc.) primarily was used. Then have your child draw a picture of your house on the square below. Please have your child return the picture to school by _____.

Thank you for your help!

Sincerely,

Name _____

My house is made of _____.

The Three Little Pigs Chant

One pig built his house of straw.
Oh, no! Oh, no!

One pig built his house of sticks.
Oh, no! Oh, no!

One pig built his house of bricks.
Smart pig! Smart pig!

Then the wolf came to blow them down.
Huff, puff! Huff, puff!

Down went the houses of straw and sticks.
Huff, puff! Huff, puff!

But he couldn't blow down that house of bricks.
Huff, puff! Huff, puff!

Who's afraid of the big bad wolf?
Not us! Not us!

Making Little Books

- -

My Little Book of
The Three Little Pigs Chant

Name_____

- -

One pig built his house of straw.
Oh, no! Oh, no!

1

- -

Making Little Books *(cont.)*

**One pig built his house of sticks.
Oh, no! Oh, no!**

2

**One pig built his house of bricks.
Smart pig! Smart pig!**

3

Making Little Books *(cont.)*

**Then the wolf came to blow them down.
Huff, puff! Huff, puff!**   **4**

**Down went the house of straw and sticks.
Huff, puff! Huff, puff!**   **5**

Making Little Books *(cont.)*

- -

**But he couldn't blow down that house
of bricks.
Huff, puff! Huff, puff!**   **6**

- -

**Who's afraid of the big bad wolf?
Not us! Not us!**   **7**

- -

Patterns

Patterns *(cont.)*

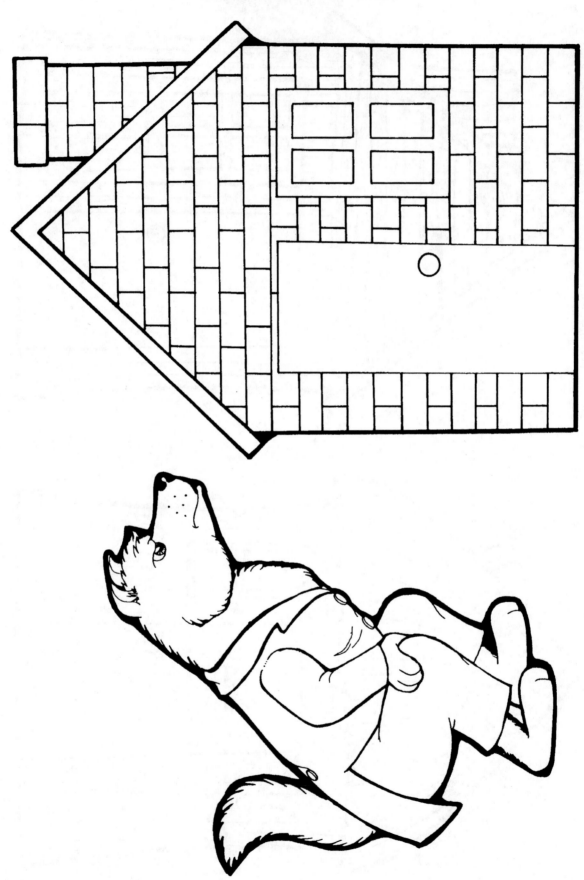

Patterns *(cont.)*

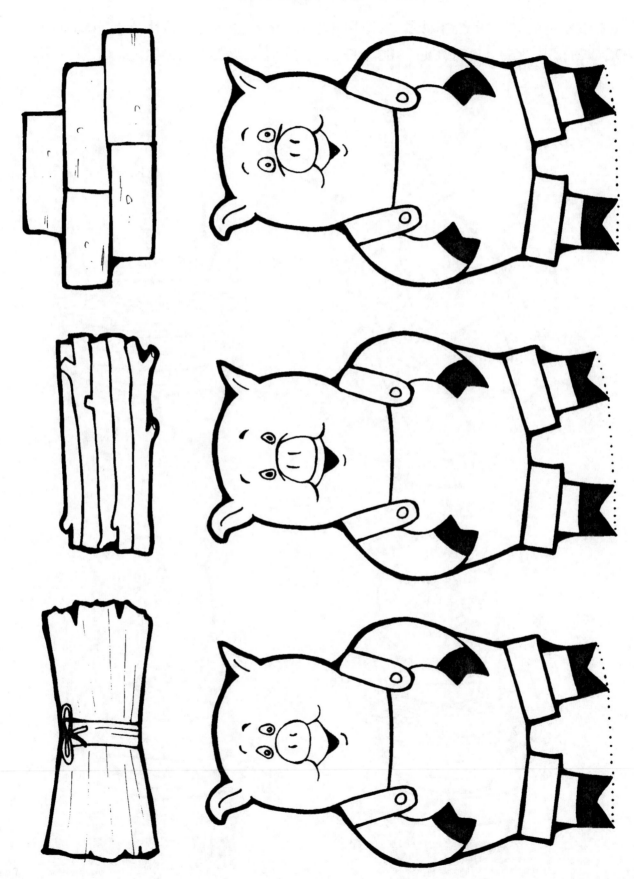

The Three Little Pigs Stick Puppets

Directions: Color and cut out these characters. Attach them to wooden sticks. Use your stick puppets to retell the story.

How to Build a House Mini-Book

How
to
Build
a
House

Name_____

Dig a hole.

Make a foundation.

Make a floor.

How to Build a House Mini-Book *(cont.)*

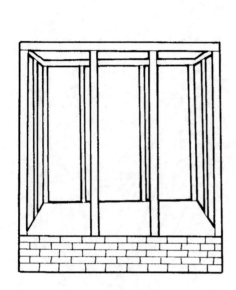

Make walls.

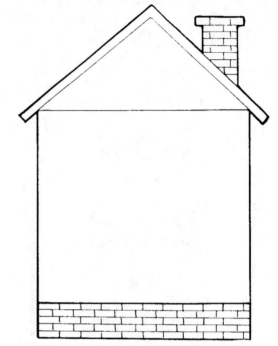

Add a roof and a chimney.

Add windows and doors.

Paint it. Move in.

Name _____

Matching Animal Homes

Directions: Draw a line from each animal to its home.

Name _____

The Three Little Pigs Story Map

Directions: Color the pictures below. Cut along the dotted lines. Glue the pictures in the correct boxes on the map to retell the story.

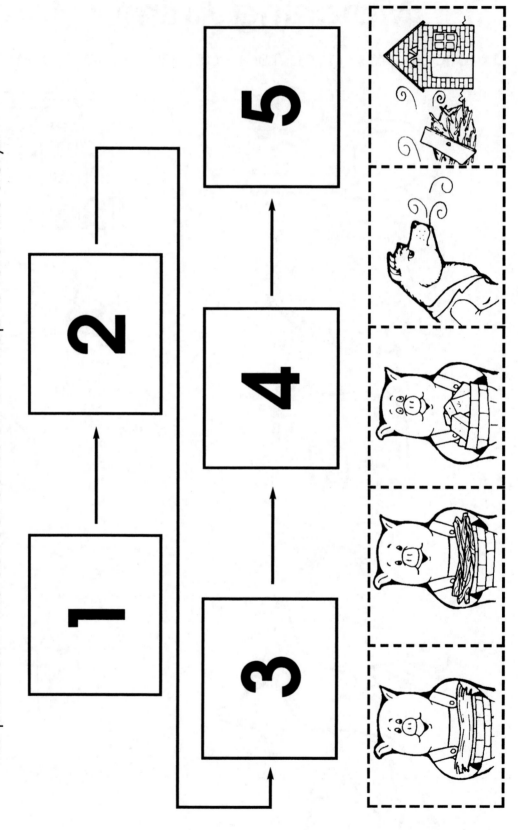

Sample Lesson Plans

Featured Literature: *The Three Billy Goats Gruff*

Author: Janet Stevens

Publisher: Harcourt Brace Jovanovich, 1987

Summary: This traditional Norwegian folktale is about three clever goats that outsmart a terrible troll who lives under a bridge. The goats illustrated in the Stevens version are especially amusing as they put on different types of clothing to fool the troll. Children will enjoy the familiar "Trip, trap" refrain in this ever popular tale.

Additional Literature: *The Three Goats* by Margaret Hillert (Follett Publishing Co., 1963); *The Three Billy-Goats Gruff* by Ellen Appleby (Scholastic, 1984); "The Three Billy Goats Gruff" by P.C. Asbjornsen from *Tomie DePaola's Favorite Nursery Tales* (G.P. Putnam's Sons, 1986); "The Three Billy Goats Gruff" from *The Three Bears & 15 Other Stories* by Anne Rockwell (Thomas Y. Crowell, 1975); *The Usborne Book of Farm Animals* by Felicity Everett (Usborne Publications, Ltd.); *Three Billy Goats Gruff* by Glen Rounds (Holiday House, 1993); *Gregory, The Terrible Eater* by Mitchell Sharmat (Four Winds Press, 1980).

Related Songs: "My Silly Billy Goat" by Susan A. Miller; "Little White Goat" by Judy Slenker, *Animal Piggyback Songs* (Warren Publishing House, 1990).

Day 1: Introduce the featured literature by writing "The Three_____ " on the chalkboard. Read the words together and ask the children to guess the title of today's story. Write down other titles suggested by the class such as "The Three Pigs" and "The Three Bears." Help the children notice how often folktales and fairytales have the number three in the title or as an important part of the plot (for example, a character has three magic wishes). Discuss the fact that *The Three Billy Goats Gruff* is a story from Norway and locate the country on a map or globe.

K	W	L
Goats have horns.	Where do goats live? What do goats really eat?	Goats eat almost anything.

Next, create a K-W-L chart, listing what the children *know* about goats on a large piece of chart paper. Then list questions the children *want* to answer about goats. Save the chart, filling in what the children have *learned* about goats later in the week.

Talk about trolls and name some other imaginary creatures found in folktales and fairy tales (fairies, witches, elves, etc.). Ask the children to predict what the troll in the book might look like. Then read the story, talking about the illustrations and pointing out that the goats are dressed like people. Reproduce the poem "The Three Billy Goats" from page 64 on a large sheet of chart paper or on an overhead transparency. Share the poem with the children, pointing at the words as you read aloud.

Send home the Parent Letter found on page 63.

Sample Lesson Plans *(cont.)*

Day 2: Prepare the "'G' Is for Goat" activity (pages 72 - 73). Start today's activities by talking about the sound that "Gg" makes. Ask the children to listen for words that begin with "Gg" as you reread yesterday's story. Then ask the children to find items in the classroom which start with "Gg" such as the globe.

Pass out picture cards to the children, some of which will show objects which begin with "Gg" and some of which show objects beginning with other letters. Tell the children that this goat will only eat pictures of things which start with "Gg." Sort the pictures and feed the goat the "Gg" pictures by placing them in the plastic pouch on his stomach. The disqualified pictures could be placed in a small, clean waste basket placed nearby.

Talk about how real goats will eat almost anything. Read facts about goats from *Usborne Book of Farm Animals* by Felicity Everett. Compare these facts to the ones listed on the K-W-L chart on Day 1. Then read the delightful story, *Gregory The Terrible Eater* by Mitchell Sharmat. In this book, a young goat named Gregory upsets his parents because he only eats people food instead of goat foods like old tin cans.

Finish the day's activities by reading *The Three Billy Goats Gruff* by Ellen Appleby, available in big book format. Compare the two versions you have read, discussing which goats looked more realistic.

Day 3: Practice reading the poem, "The Three Billy Goats." Reproduce the little book of the poem (pages 65 - 68) and have the children color, cut, and assemble it. Read the book together several times, emphasizing the repetitive phrases. Send the book home at the end of the week for children to share.

Write some of the phrases from the story on sentence strips such as "Who's that tripping across my bridge?" and "Trip, trap, trip, trap". Put the sentences in the pocket chart and read them together. The sentences can also be held up by students as the story is read.

Read "The Three Billy Goats Gruff" from *DePaola's Favorite Nursery Tales*. Talk about how this book is an anthology, meaning that it contains a collection of many favorite tales.

Reproduce the bridge and characters found on pages 69 - 71 on tagboard. Have the children color and cut out the pieces for use as a story retelling kit. After practicing the story at school, children also can take this activity home to share with their parents.

Sample Lesson Plans *(cont.)*

Day 4: Read *The Three Goats* by Margaret Hillert. Look at the bridges in all the versions you have read and discuss how they are the same or different. Discuss why bridges are built and ask the children to name bridges found in the area in which you live. Obtain some pictures from the library of famous bridges such as the Golden Gate Bridge in San Francisco and the Ambassador Bridge that links Michigan and Canada. Save the pictures for use in the Block Center.

Invite an engineer to come to your class as a guest speaker to talk about the construction of bridges. Children will be most interested if they can see blueprints, slides, tools or building materials used in construction.

There are many words that begin with blends or consonant clusters in this story such as bridge, trip, and snip. If reading blends is a skill you need to teach in your classroom, this is a good opportunity for teaching them in context. Have the children brainstorm a list of other words that start with the blends tr, br, sn, and others. For a listening game, make small cards with the blends written on them and pass them out to the class. Say a word or show a picture of an object that begins with one of the blends. Students display the card when they see a word that starts with the blend they are holding.

Extend your students' learning by introducing the Learning Centers for this theme. See page 62 for some ideas.

Day 5: As part of the concluding activities, prepare a drawing of a simple barn shape on a large piece of paper and start today's activities by brainstorming a list of farm animals on the shape. Then introduce the farm riddles found on page 74.

One idea for a culminating activity would be to visit a farm to see some real goats. If you cannot visit a farm, bring in some goat milk and goat cheese for the children to sample and compare to cow's milk and cheese. Make a simple graph by dividing a large sheet of bulletin board paper into columns, one for each cheese tasted. Label columns and have the children sign their name under their favorite cheese.

Another possibility for a culminating activity is to have a "Country Fair." Children can be invited to bring in stuffed animals to enter in the fair. Award each animal a blue ribbon for participation. Have each child tell why their animal deserves a second blue ribbon for being the biggest, the cutest, etc.. Finish the fair with a pie tasting or a pie eating contest.

Sample Centers

Reading Center: Have available all of the literature used throughout this unit. Also provide multiple copies of the little books of the poem and a large copy of the poem on chart paper. Post lists of words which start with any blends or consonant clusters you worked on during the week. Make a laminated copy of the "'G' Is for Goat" game introduced this week so that children may practice sorting pictures by initial sound.

Another sorting activity can be made by providing an enlarged picture of a goat with "Gg" and a troll "Tt" printed under the figure. Put out magazines, picture cards, or old phonics books and have the children cut out pictures which begin with these two letters to be sorted into two piles placed on the goat and troll.

Writing Center: Have each child contribute a page for a barn shaped book about farm animals. Post the list of farm animals brainstormed by the children on Day 5. Have them complete the sentence frame "A _____ is a farm animal" across the bottom of the page and then illustrate the sentence with marker or crayon. Put the completed book at the reading center or the classroom library.

Math Center: Set up a measurement center designed to reinforce the concepts of size covered in the story. Make available materials such as interlocking plastic blocks and ask children to build "towers" or "trains." They can then arrange these structures in order from shortest to longest or shortest to tallest.

Ask the children to bring in toy trolls to be sorted by size. Fill your Estimating Jar with small trolls. Have the children estimate how many trolls there are, counting to check their guesses.

Art Center: Children may paint goats to be placed around a large bridge displayed on a bulletin board. Make a speech bubble for each goat to show what it would say to the troll. Don't forget to put a troll under the bridge!

Science Center: Put out a model barn and small model farm animals. Write the names of the animals on cards for a matching activity. Add a display of non-fiction books about farm animals.

Block Center: Encourage the children to build bridges with a variety of building materials such as wood building blocks and plastic interconnecting blocks. Stimulate interest by displaying pictures of famous bridges shown on Day 3.

Parent Letter

Dear Parents,

We are beginning a new unit of literature study featuring *The Three Billy Goats Gruff.* Our main selection will be a colorful version of this classic Norwegian folktale adapted and illustrated by Janet Stevens. Other versions of the story such as the one by Ellen Appleby also will be read for comparison.

We will cover many curriculum areas in this unit. Here's a preview of what we have planned:

1. Learning about goats and other farm animals in our science center.
2. Arranging items in order of length and size as this concept of measurement is important in the story.
3. Talking about the sound made by the letter "Gg."

Thank you for your cooperation in helping your child to learn!

Sincerely,

- -

Name_____

Please help your child to write a word that begins with the letter "Gg" as heard in the word "goat". Have your child draw a picture in the box to illustrate the word and return this to school by _____.

G is for _____.

The Three Goats

The three goats are hungry
For something to eat.
Trip, trap
Trip, trap.

But under the bridge
Watch out for the troll!
Trip, trap
Trip, trap.

Over the bridge
The little goat crosses.
Trip, trap
Trip, trap.

Over the bridge
The second goat crosses.
Trip, trap
Trip, trap.

Over the bridge
The biggest goat crosses.
Trip, trap
Trip, trap.

Off the bridge goes the troll
And the goats have their lunch.
Trip, trap
Trip, trap.

The three goats' story
Has come to an end.
Snip, snap, snout
This tale's told out.

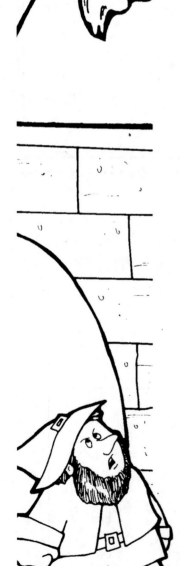

64

Making Little Books

- -

My Little Book of
The Three Billy Goats

Name_____

- -

The three goats are hungry
For something to eat,
Trip, trap, Trip, trap.

1

- -

Making Little Books *(cont.)*

But under the bridge
Watch out for the troll!
Trip, trap, trip, trap.   **2**

Over the bridge
The little goat crosses.
Trip, trap, trip, trap.   **3**

Making Little Books *(cont.)*

**Over the bridge
The second goat crosses.
Trip, trap, trip, trap.**

4

**Over the bridge
The biggest goat crosses.
Trip, trap, trip, trap.**

5

Making Little Books *(cont.)*

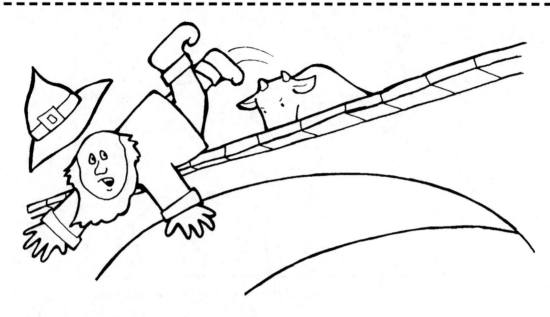

Off the bridge goes the troll
And the goats have their lunch.
Trip, trap, trip, trap.   6

The three goats' story
Has come to an end.
Snip, snap, snout,
This tale's told out.   7

Make a Bridge

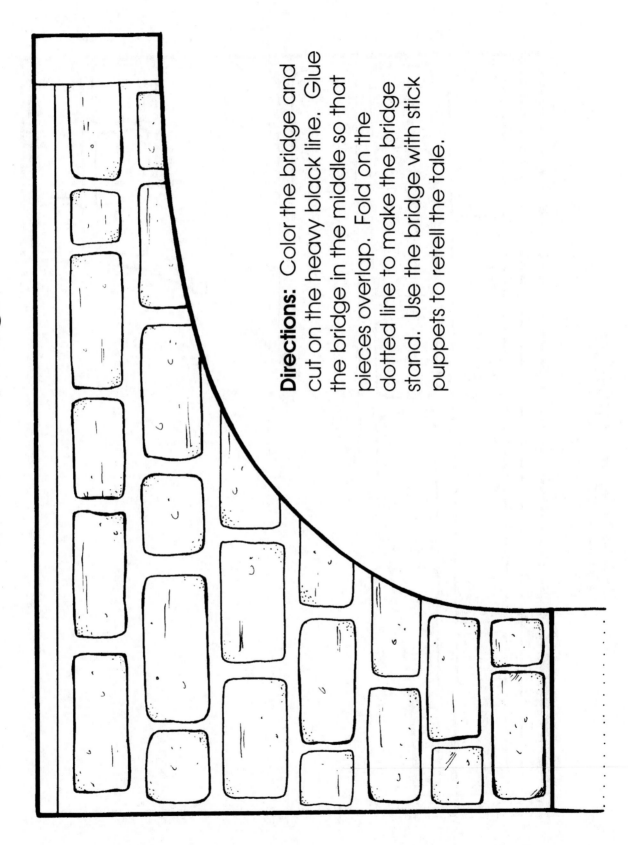

Directions: Color the bridge and cut on the heavy black line. Glue the bridge in the middle so that pieces overlap. Fold on the dotted line to make the bridge stand. Use the bridge with stick puppets to retell the tale.

Make a Bridge *(cont.)*

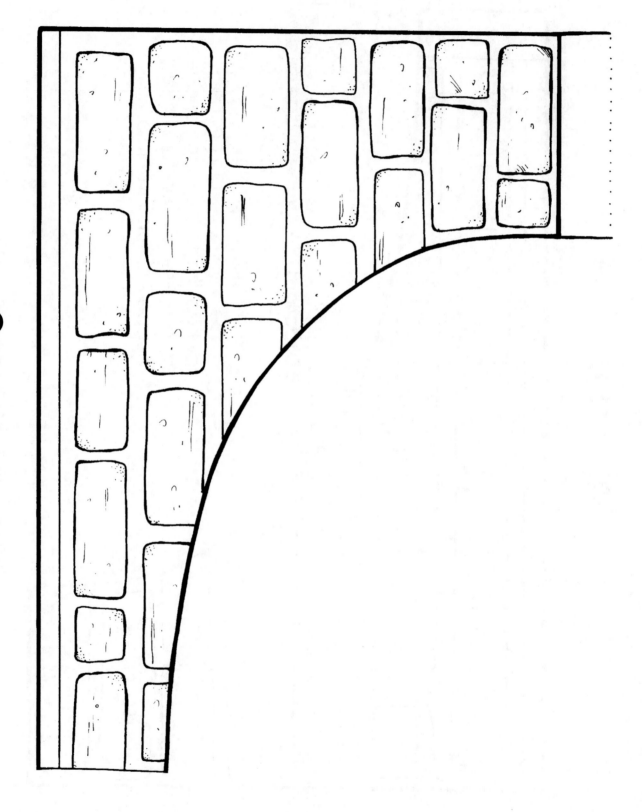

Character Patterns

Directions: Color and cut out these characters. Staple them to wooden sticks. Use for retelling the story with the bridge you have made.

"G" Is For Goat

Teacher's Directions: Color the goat, cut it out and the pocket, and laminate both. Attach the pocket to the goat and use it to hold the picture cards of objects which begin with "Gg" from page 73.

Pocket

"G" Is for Goat Picture Cards

Farm Riddles

Teacher's Directions: Use these riddles along with the flannel board figures to review types of farm animals.

A pen is my home
In the mud I play.
I'm round and fat
I can eat all day.
What am I?

Hatching from an egg
Soft and yellow.
Soon I'll be
A fluffy fellow.
What am I?

I chew my cud
And swish my tail.
My delicious milk
Goes into a pail.
What am I?

Fleecy and soft
My wool is for you.
To make into sweaters.
And mittens too.
What am I?

Chasing the mice
Around the barn.
Then just for fun
I play with yarn.
What am I?

74

Patterns for Farm Riddles

Sample Lesson Plans

Featured Literature: *The Little Red Hen*

Retold and illustrated by: Lucinda McQueen

Publisher: Scholastic, Inc., 1985

Summary: This book tells the classic story of Little Red Hen who planted grains of wheat, cared for it, took it to the mill to be ground into flour, and baked the flour into bread all by herself. Her three friends (the goose, the cat, and the dog) refuse to help and miss out on eating the bread baked by the hen at the end of the story.

Additional Literature: *The Little Red Hen* by Paul Galdone (Houghton Mifflin, 1973); *The Little Red Hen* by Karen Schmidt (Grosset & Dunlap, 1984); *The Little Red Hen* by Margot Zemach (Farrar, Strauss & Giroux, 1983); *The Little Yellow Chicken* by Joy Cowley (The Wright Group, 19201 120th Avenue NE, Bothell, WA 98011-9512; phone [800] 345-6073); *Chick* by Jane Burton (Dorling Kindersley, 1991); *Bread, Bread, Bread* by Ann Morris (Lothrop, 1989)

Related Songs: "I'm a Little Chicken" by Susan Peters, *Holiday Piggyback Songs* (Warren Publishing House, 1988); "Look at All the Chickens" by Cindy Dingwell and "The Chicken Family" by Carla C. Skjong, *Animal Piggyback Songs* (Warren Publishing House, 1990).

Day 1: Introduce the story of *The Little Red Hen* to your class while holding a red hen puppet in your lap. (A red hen puppet is available from Folkmania, Inc., 1219 Park Avenue, Emeryville, CA 94608; phone [510] 658-7677.) This puppet may be held by the children during each reading and then placed in your reading center for children to use independently in their retellings. Then read the McQueen version of *The Little Red Hen* to your class, inviting your students to join in on the "Not I!" refrain. Use your hand under the words as you are reading, and have children point to the "Not I!" sections.

After reading the story, ask questions such as, "Is this is a real or make-believe story? How can you tell? What do you think the goose, cat, and dog should have done? What needs to be done in a garden? Have you ever grown something in a garden? What lesson did the goose, cat, and dog learn in the story? What are some ways that you help at your house?"

Prepare the flannel board shapes from the patterns on pages 86 - 89 to retell the story on your flannel board. Place the shapes and the flannel board in your reading center for children to use in their own independent retellings.

Reproduce the poem "Little Red Hen" from page 81 on a large sheet of chart paper or on an overhead transparency.   Read the poem, asking children to join in on the "Not I!" refrain. Make sentence strips of the poem to use in a pocket chart for practicing sequencing skills. Put the strips and your pocket chart at your Reading Center for independent reading practice.

Sample Lesson Plans *(cont.)*

Day 1, *cont.*: Use a disposable cup for each child to plant grains of wheat or grass seed. Write the child's name on the cup, put a hole in the bottom for drainage, and fill each cup with soil to within an inch (cm) of the top. Give each child about twenty seeds to put on top of the soil, then cover seeds with just enough soil to hide them. Water the seeds and place them in a sunny location in your classroom, ideally at your Science Center.

Send home the Parent Letter on page 80.

Day 2: Reread the McQueen version of *The Little Red Hen* and have volunteers dramatize the story as you are reading. Make a sentence strip card that says "Who will help me?" for the child playing the Little Red Hen to display and read at the appropriate time. Similarly, make sentence strip cards for the goose, cat, and dog to display and read for the "Not I!" refrain. Children who are not involved in dramatizing may read along with the actors.

Reread the "Little Red Hen" poem with the children. Reproduce pages 82 to 85 for the children to color, cut, and assemble their own little books of the poem. Practice the poem many times during the week and send home the books with the children at the end of the week to share at home.

Day 3: Read two other versions of *The Little Red Hen* today. The Galdone and Schmidt versions would be good ones for comparing and contrasting with the McQueen version. Make a new Comparison Chart, affixing copies of the covers from books you have read thus far across the top of a large sheet of bulletin board paper. Be sure to leave room for adding two additional titles later. Along the side of the chart list elements for the children to compare such as the characters included, who worked and who did not, who eats the bread, etc.

Grass and wheat seeds grow rapidly, so check them today to see if they are sprouting. Use a Science Journal format (page 144) to record the childrens' observations.

Day 4: Begin today by reading yet another version of *The Little Red Hen*, such as the one by Margot Zemach. Compare and contrast this version to the ones previously read, adding the book cover and recording information on the chart you created yesterday.

Have the children color and cut the character patterns on page 90 to create their own set of finger puppets to use in retelling the story. Children may practice retelling the story in pairs and then take the finger puppets home to share the story with their parents.

As a final activity for today, ask your students if the story of the Little Red Hen is about real animals or pretend animals and to state their reasons. If the children are unsure, build their prior knowledge by reading a sampling of books about real farm animals. *Chick* by Jane Burton is an excellent resource for this purpose. Non-fiction books, magazine articles and posters about farm animals can be kept in your Science Center. Don't forget to have children check their seeds and record their observations.

Sample Lesson Plans *(cont.)*

Day 4, cont.: Extend the students' learning by introducing the Learning Centers for this theme. See page 79 for some ideas.

Day 5: As your culminating activity for this unit, plan a bread-making day. Use your favorite recipe for whole wheat bread or follow the one on page 92 . Enlarge the recipe on a large sheet of chart paper or on an overhead transparency to display for the children while you are making the bread. Begin with an integrated math lesson by having the children sit on the floor in a circle while you demonstrate how to measure and add ingredients to a large mixing bowl, introducing the concept of fractions. Individual children may help you to add the ingredients.

As you are making your bread, emphasize the amount of hard work involved. Draw parallels between your bread-making project with the Little Red Hen's bread-making experience, for example, correlating the whole wheat flour you are using with the wheat that the Little Red Hen had ground into flour at the mill. Encourage discussion with questions such as, "Is it easier to make bread with the help of friends than it is to make it alone?" and "How do you think the Little Red Hen felt about having to do all of this hard work by herself?"

As your bread is rising, read the nonfiction book *Bread, Bread, Bread* by Ann Morris about breads around the world. Use your globe to locate the countries where various types of bread can be found to heighten your students' awareness of other cultures and to introduce basic geography. You also could provide several different kinds of bread such as French bread, pita bread, rye bread, etc., for your students to sample during today's bread feast. For independent study, put *Bread, Bread, Bread* at your Social Studies Center along with a globe or world map.

As your final version of this classic tale, read a book with a twist. *The Little Yellow Chicken* by Joy Cowley tells what happens when the Little Red Hen's grandson faces a dilemma similar to his grandmother's.

Create a class graph of the childrens' favorite version of the tale by writing the title of each book across the top of a large sheet of paper. Children may write their own names under the title of their favorite version. Reread the class' favorite version one more time as your students enjoy a bread feast.

Sample Centers

Reading Center: Display copies of all versions of *The Little Red Hen* shared in class, plus all nonfiction selections. Invite children to retell the story using the flannel board or finger puppets. Make several extra copies of the "Little Red Hen" poem and little books for use in this center.

Make copies of page 91 for children to use in sequencing the main events in the story. You may add a cover and staple the pages into booklets, or you may add a title and display on strips of 3" x 18" (20 cm x 100 cm) construction paper at your center. The sentences from this page may be enlarged on sentence strips and used for sequencing in a pocket chart.

Writing Center: Children can make individual story maps of their favorite story version using words and pictures on large sheets of construction paper. Be sure that you have modeled how a story map is made beforehand so that children may work independently.

Math Center: Put wheat grains or grass seed into your Estimating Jar. For reference, place ten seeds or grains into an identical jar. Discuss with your students the tiny amount of area taken up by ten seeds and discuss whether their estimates should be more than, less than, or equal to ten. Limit the number of seeds in the estimating jar to fifty or less to facilitate accurate guessing.

For practice in measuring, fill a large tub with wheat grains or grass seed. Provide a variety of containers, spoons, and measuring cups for children to use in experimenting with volume.

Science Center: Display non-fiction books, magazine articles, and posters about real farm animals at this center for the children to extend their learning independently.

The wheat or grass plantings may be kept here and observed daily by the children. Children may write their scientific observations in journals. Make available books about growing plants, hand lenses, and rules for watching and measuring the growth of the seedlings.

Social Studies Center: Keep several copies of *Bread, Bread, Bread,* your classroom globe, and a world map at this center to use in locating the countries where various breads are made and eaten.

Dramatic Play Center: Have a variety of kitchen and gardening supplies available for children to use in pretending to grow wheat and make bread. Items such as a plastic hoe, watering can, plastic wheelbarrow, sack, apron, mixing bowl, wooden spoon, and bread pans would be appropriate.

Art Center: Paper plates and scraps can be used by the children to create masks of the characters. Staple masks to wooden sticks to hold during retellings of the story.

Parent Letter

Dear Parents,

Our class is now working on a thematic unit based upon the classic tale, *The Little Red Hen*. Our activites related to this tale will extend across the curriculum. Plan to discuss with your child what we have learned each day. Your child will be bringing home a little book of a poem, "The Little Red Hen" to read with you. We have several fun learning experiences planned:

1. Making a chart to record how the different versions of *The Little Red Hen* are alike and different.
2. Making finger puppets of the characters and using them to retell the story.
3. Working together to make our own whole wheat bread.

Since the Little Red Hen was not able to get help to plant wheat or bake bread, one concept we will be working to develop is the importance of working together and helping others. Please discuss the ways in which your child works with others to help at your house. Then have your child draw and write about helping others in the bottom section of this page. Please see that your child returns this to school by _____ .

Thank you for your help and cooperation with this lesson on teamwork!

Sincerely,

My Name is _____. I help by _____.

The Little Red Hen

Little Red Hen has found some wheat.
"Who will help me plant the wheat,
so we may have bread to eat?"
"Not I!" "Not I!" "Not I!"

"Who will help me water the wheat,
so we may have bread to eat?"
"Not I!" "Not I!" "Not I!"

"Who will help me hoe the wheat,
so we may have bread to eat?"
"Not I!" "Not I!" "Not I!"

"Who will help me cut the wheat,
so we may have bread to eat?"
"Not I!" "Not I!" "Not I!"

"Who will help me grind the wheat,
so we may have bread to eat?"
"Not I!" "Not I!" "Not I!"

"Who will help me make the bread?"
"Not I!" "Not I!" "Not I!" her friends all said.

Her friends all wanted to eat.
But Little Red Hen ate the whole treat!

Making Little Books

- -

My Little Book of
The Little Red Hen

Name_____

- -

**Little Red Hen has found some wheat.
"Who will help me plant the wheat,
so we may have bread to eat?"
"Not I!" "Not I!" "Not I!"**

1

- -

Making Little Books *(cont.)*

**"Who will help me water the wheat,
so we may have bread to eat?"
"Not I!" "Not I!" Not I!"**

2

**"Who will help me hoe the wheat,
so we may have bread to eat?"
"Not I!" "Not I!" "Not I!"**

3

Making Little Books *(cont.)*

"Who will help me cut the wheat,
so we may have bread to eat?"
"Not I!" "Not I!" "Not I!"   4

"Who will help me grind the wheat,
so we may have bread to eat?"
"Not I!" "Not I!" "Not I!"   5

Making Little Books *(cont.)*

"Who will help me make the bread?"
"Not I!" "Not I!" "Not I!" her friends
all said.   **6**

Her friends all wanted to eat.
But Little Red Hen ate the whole treat!   **7**

Patterns

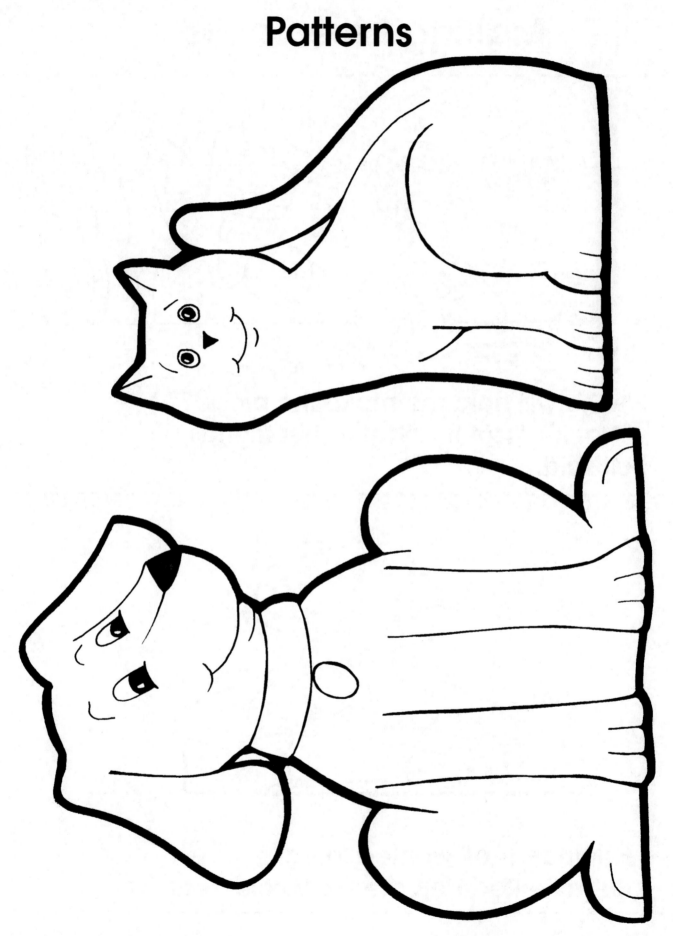

Patterns *(cont.)*

Patterns *(cont.)*

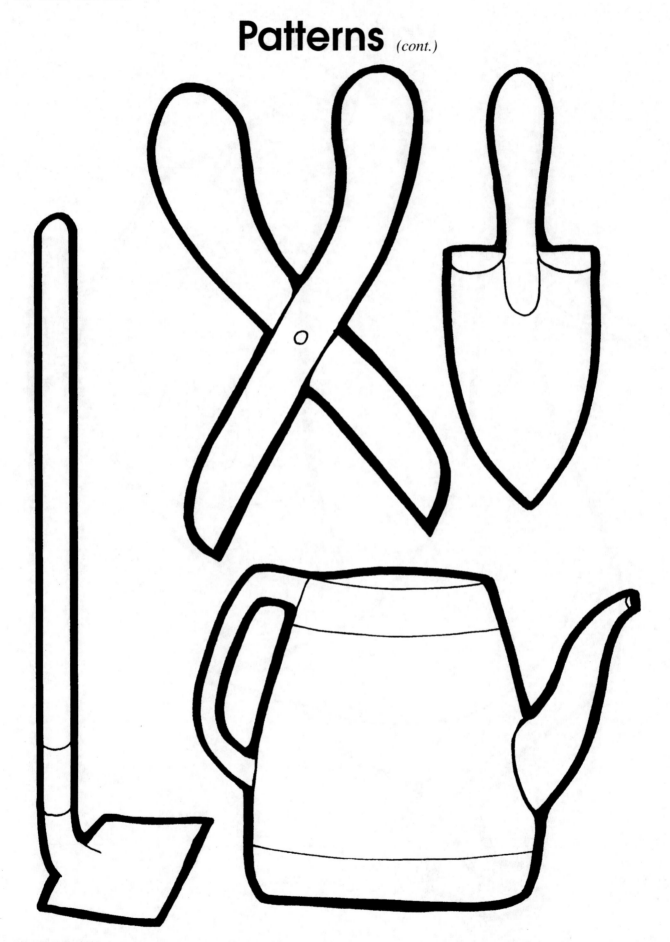

Patterns *(cont.)*

Finger Puppet Patterns

Story Sequencing

Directions: Color and cut the pictures along the dotted lines. Then arrange the pictures in the correct sequence.

The Little Red Hen watered the wheat.

The Little Red Hen ate the bread.

The Little Red Hen made the bread.

The Little Red Hen found some wheat.

The Little Red Hen planted the wheat.

The Little Red Hen cut the wheat.

Whole Wheat Bread Recipe
(Makes 2 loaves)

Ingredients:

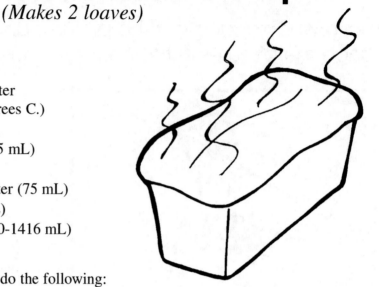

- 2 packages active dry yeast
- 2¼ cups (540mL) very warm water
  (105-115 degrees F., 40-45 degrees C.)
- ⅓ cup honey (75 mL)
- ⅓ cup instant nonfat dry milk (75 mL)
- 4 t. salt (20 mL)
- ⅓ cup softened margarine or butter (75 mL)
- 2 cups all-purpose flour (472 mL)
- 5-6 cups whole wheat flour (1180-1416 mL)

Teacher Directions

Gather your students around you as you do the following:

1. Put the warm water and honey into a large mixing bowl. Add yeast and stir briefly. Let stand for 2 minutes.
2. Add instant dry milk and salt and stir.
3. Add softened margarine, all-purpose flour, and 2 cups (472 mL) of the whole wheat flour. Stir the dough until it looks smooth, then beat for an additional 2 minutes.
4. Mix in enough of the remaining whole wheat flour to make a soft dough.
5. Prepare a surface using the remaining whole wheat flour and place the dough on it for kneading.

Student Directions

1. Take turns using the heels of your hands to knead the dough for a total of 5 minutes. Add a little flour as needed to keep dough from sticking to the surface.
2. Butter the inside of a bowl.
3. Put the dough inside the bowl. Turn the dough over so that the buttered side is on top.
4. Cover with clear plastic wrap and put the bowl in a warm place.
5. After about an hour, check to see if the dough looks twice as big as when you put it in the bowl. If the dough has risen, proceed with the recipe. If not, put the bowl back in the warm spot and wait.

Teacher Directions

Gather your students around you as you do the following:

1. Butter two 8½" x 4 ½" x 2 ½" loaf pans (22 cm x 11 cm x 6 cm)
2. Punch down the dough after it has risen. Put the dough on a floured surface. Cut the dough in half and shape each half into a loaf. Put loaves into pans. Cover with clear plastic wrap. Let rise in a warm spot for about 30 minutes until about doubled in size.
3. Put pans into an unheated oven. Turn oven on to 400 degrees F (204° C).
4. Bake 35-40 minutes. Cool.

Teacher and Student Directions

1. Slice the bread. Add butter, if desired.
2. Eat and ENJOY!

Sample Lesson Plans

Featured Literature: *The Gingerbread Man*

Author: Eric A. Kimmel

Publisher: Holiday House, 1993

Summary: As the gingerbread man runs, he meets a variety of animals that can't stop him until he encounters a clever and hungry fox. This version of the story has an interesting twist, with the hope that more gingerbread men will appear in the future whenever someone chooses to bake them.

Additional Literature: *The Gingerbread Man* by Richard Scarry (Western Publishing Company, 1975); *The Gingerbread Man* by Karen Schmidt (Scholastic, 1967); *The Gingerbread Boy* by David Cutts (Troll Associates, 1979); *The Fine Round Cake* by Arnica Esterl (Macmillan Publisher Company, 1991.

Related Songs: "Gingerbread Boy" and "Gingerbread" by Joyce Marshall, *More Piggyback Songs* (Warren Publishing House, 1984).

Day 1: Start this unit with a guessing game. Prepare the game by reproducing and cutting apart a gingerbread shape (pattern on page 102). On each of the legs, arms, body and head, write one of the following clues:

1. This story has many characters.
2. This story has animals in it.
3. This story will make you hungry.
4. This story has a character who likes to run.
5. This story has something to do with cookies.
6. This story starts with an old woman.

Tell the children that you are going to read a favorite tale and that you will give them some clues for guessing the story's title. As the clues are read, re-assemble the gingerbread man, beginning with the body and adding the legs, arms, and head.

Once children have guessed the title, read the main selection, predicting what animal might appear next. Encourage the children to join in on the repeating phrases. After reading, discuss the unusual ending and encourage ideas for a different story ending by asking questions such as, what if the fox had not eaten the gingerbread man? What might have happened next?

As a treat when you finish reading the story, give each student a round peppermint candy, representing the gingerbread man's buttons. Have the children enjoy their candies while you read "The Gingerbread Man" poem to the class, reproduced on a large sheet of chart paper or on an overhead transparency (see page 97).

Send home the Parent Letter found on page 96.

Sample Lesson Plans *(cont.)*

Day 2: Practice reading "The Gingerbread Man" poem together, pointing to the words as you read. Have some volunteers come up and point to some of the repetitive words such as "run," "fast," and "man".

Then read *The Gingerbread* Man by Karen Schmidt, comparing this book to yesterday's version. Discuss how the animals in Schmidt's version are dressed like people. Prepare a Comparison Chart on a large piece of bulletin board paper. Affix a copy of the cover from both versions across the top, leaving room to add other versions you will be reading. Along the side list questions such as, are there characters common to all the stories? Do all the characters look like real animals or are they dressed like people?

Day 3: After practicing "The Gingerbread Man" poem, have the children cut, color, and assemble their own little books of the poem (pages 98 - 101). Practice reading the little books together and send them home at the end of the week to share.

Read either the Scarry or Cutts version of the story, or share the classic English fairy tale, *The Fine Round Cake*. Add new information to your Comparison Chart.

Give children the opportunity to create fancy gingerbread people. Use the pattern on page 102 to trace gingerbread people on brown construction paper. Have the children cut out the tracing and then use construction paper and other materials from your Art Center to create facial features and a costume. (If you are working on this unit at Christmas time, the children can make gingerbread angels, reindeer, Santas, and so on. The gingerbread people also make nice Christmas tree decorations along with colorful paper chains. Complete the tree with a gingerbread angel at the top.)

Day 4: Make a large mural for retelling the story. After covering a bulletin board with paper, a paper cottage and characters can be pinned along a paper road. Children can move a paper gingerbread man along the road as they retell his adventures.

Extend your activities by introducing Learning Centers for this theme. Some ideas can be found on page 95.

Day 5: Culminate this unit by having a "Cookie Day," either baking and decorating your own gingerbread people or using some of the recipes sent in by parents. Some cookies also could be donated to a local senior citizen home or homeless shelter.

Finally, reproduce the parents' recipes and assemble them into booklets. Let children make their own covers, and send home the recipe book as a keepsake of their gingerbread week.

Sample Centers

Reading Center: Have a copy of the main selection available and make a display of the other versions of the stories read during the week, perhaps setting the books on a counter or shelf with a stuffed gingerbread character. (You can usually find gingerbread toys around Christmas time or else sew one easily by using the gingerbread pattern on page 102). Use the patterns on pages 103 to 106 to make flannel board characters for retelling the story. Display other materials used during the week, including the comparison chart, copies of the little books, and a chart or transparency of the gingerbread poem.

Prepare the "Gingerbread Man Game Board" for use at this center by copying pages 107 to 108 and gluing the game into a file folder before laminating it. You will also need to make small gingerbread man shaped playing pieces from construction paper. In small groups ahead of time, teach the children how to play the game or have a parent helper available at the center. The purpose of the game is to help children recall the plot in sequence.

Writing Center: Invite the children to make up their own cookie recipes on recipe cards provided by you. They could begin by making a list of ingredients and then writing the directions using invented spelling. Another idea is for children to write letters to the Gingerbread Man, advising him how to outsmart the fox. If possible, have a parent volunteer edit the finished letters. Provide the children with a variety of stationery for copying their final drafts.

Math Center: If you have a sand or water table, use it with this unit to practice estimation and measurement. Talk about the measurements used in baking such as teaspoon and cup (or mL and L) and provide a variety of plastic jars, spoons, cups, and scoops. If you do not have a table, children can measure rice and sand placed in a large tub.

Fill your Estimating Jar with round peppermint candies. Have children estimate the contents and then count the candy to check their guesses. No eating!

Art Center: Provide several colors of dough or clay, cookie cutters and cookie sheets for children to create their favorite pretend cookies. They can "bake" their treats in the Dramatic Play Center.

Dramatic Play Center: Set up this area as the "Gingerbread Bakery Shop." Provide props such as baking utensils, a play oven, chef hats, a cash register with play money, and bakery boxes or bags. Encourage the children to make a large sign advertising the bakery as well as smaller signs announcing the prices of baked goods or sales. They can also make a list of the types of baked goods the bakery offers for sale. The signs also could be made at the Writing Center and brought to use here.

Parent Letter

Dear Parents,

We are beginning a new literature unit this week, The Gingerbread Man. Our featured version will be *The Gingerbread Man* by Eric A. Kimmel. We will be reading several versions of this folktale to compare. In addition to making little books of "The Gingerbread Man" poem, our activities will cover many curriculum areas. Here are some of the things we will be doing:

1. Making a mural to retell the story.

2. Writing our own unique cookie recipes.

3. Learning about measurement as we bake various cookies.

4. Setting up a pretend bakery in our Dramatic Play Center.

We need your help in assembling a class recipe book. Please write your favorite cookie recipe on the card provided below and return it to school by _____. All the parents' recipes will be compiled and a booklet will be sent home with your child. Thanks for your help in this project!

Sincerely,

My Favorite Recipe For Cookies

From the kitchen of _____.

_____

_____

_____

_____

_____

_____

_____

The Gingerbread Man

Run, run
As fast as you can.
You can't catch me,
I'm the gingerbread man!

Here come the old woman
And the old man.
Run, run
As fast as you can.

Here comes a pig,
Mr. Gingerbread Man.
Run, run
As fast as you can.

Here comes a dog,
Mr. Gingerbread Man.
Run, run
As fast as you can.

Here comes a horse,
Mr. Gingerbread Man.
Run, run
As fast as you can.

Here comes a cow,
Mr. Gingerbread Man.
Run, run
As fast as you can.

Run, run
As fast as you can.
But the fox caught you,
Mr. Gingerbread Man!

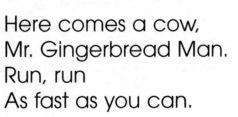

Making Little Books

My Little Book of
The Gingerbread Man

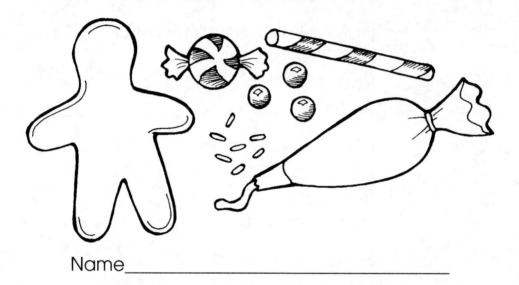

Name_____

**Run, run
As fast as you can.
You can't catch me,
I'm the gingerbread man!**

1

Making Little Book *(cont.)*

Here come the old woman
And the old man.
Run, run
As fast as you can.

2

Here comes a pig
Mr. Gingerbread Man.
Run, run
As fast as you can.

3

Making Little Book

Here comes a dog,
Mr. Gingerbread Man.
Run, run
As fast as you can.   **4**

Here comes a horse,
Mr. Gingerbread Man.
Run, run
As fast as you can.   **5**

Making Little Book *(cont.)*

Here comes a cow,
Mr. Gingerbread Man.
Run, run
As fast as you can.

6

Run, run
As fast as you can.
But the fox caught you,
Mr. Gingerbread Man!

7

Gingerbread Man Pattern

Patterns *(cont.)*

Patterns *(cont.)*

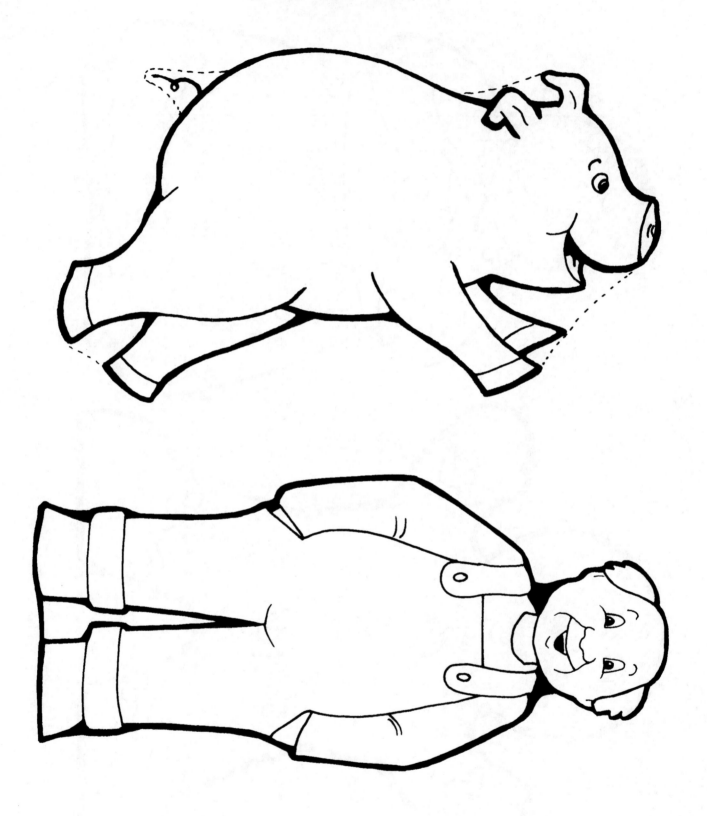

Patterns *(cont.)*

Patterns *(cont.)*

Gingerbread Man Gameboard

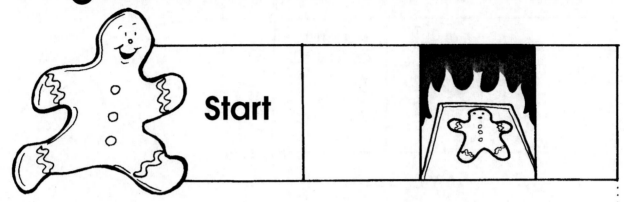

Start

Directions: Roll a die to find out how many spaces to move your gingerbread man. Tell the story events as you land on the squares. The winner is the child who reaches the gingerbread house first.

You are getting tired. Go back two spaces.

Gingerbread Man Gameboard *(cont.)*

Sample Lesson Plans

Featured Literature: *The Hare and the Tortoise*

Retold by: Caroline Castle

Publisher: Dial Books for Young Readers, 1985

Summary: This favorite fable tells of the over-confident hare and the hard-working tortoise that hold a race between them with a surprise winner.

Additional Literature: *The Hare and the Tortoise* illustrated by Brian Wildsmith (Oxford University Press, 1966); *The Tortoise and the Hare* adapted and illustrated by Janet Stevens (Holiday House, 1984); "The Tortoise and the Hare" by Aesop, *Tomie DePaola's Favorite Nursery Tales,* illustrated by Tomie DePaola (G.P. Putnam's Sons, 1986); *See How They Grow* series (Dorling Kindersley).

Related Songs: "Turtle in Your Shell" by Betty Silkunas and "See the Fluffy Rabbit" by Susan M. Paprocki, *Animal Piggyback Songs* (Warren Publishing House, 1990).

Day 1: Introduce this fable to your class by explaining that a fable is a story in which animal characters act and speak like people and also usually help us learn a lesson. Then introduce the hare and the tortoise as being similar to a rabbit and a turtle. Ask your students what they know about the way rabbits and turtles move. Do they know which animal moves faster? Have one student volunteer show how a rabbit moves and another student volunteer show how a turtle moves.

Now read the humorous Castle version of this fable. Since Badger sells tickets to the race for a penny apiece, give each child a ticket reproduced from page 121 as a story souvenir when you finish reading.

Encourage children to look at the illustrations carefully to identify the many types of animals in the book. Make a list of these animals and discuss whether they look real or make-believe. Ask the children to tell you how they know.

Make a story map. Use a large piece of brown bulletin board paper, about 3' x 3' (91 cm x 91 cm), as the background. Then draw a race track over the paper to use as the basis for the map. Add signs for the race track that say "START" and another that says "FINISH LINE." Children can use scraps of construction paper and crayons to make pieces of scenery and characters for the story. Lay the background on the floor and have children glue on their additions around the track. Make labels showing how the race progressed, using phrases such as "from the starting line," "over the hill," "across the meadow," "along the molehills," and "to the finish line."

Begin a Comparison Chart today to compare the different versions of *The Hare and the Tortoise.* As before, make copies of the covers of books you will be reading and place them across the top of a large sheet of bulletin board paper. Questions to write along the side of the chart might include, who were the main characters? Who won the race? How was the tortoise able to win? What was unique about each version? Record the childrens' answers on the chart.

Use the flannel board patterns on pages 119 – 120 to make shapes for use in retelling the story. Keep these at your Reading Center so that the children may use them independently for their retellings.

Send home the Parent Letter on page 113.

Sample Lesson Plans *(cont.)*

Day 2: Ask your children if they remember the fable that they heard yesterday, then have them practice orally retelling it. Call on students one by one to retell the story for the class, giving the students prompts as needed.

Read a different version of the tale today such as "The Tortoise and the Hare" found in the DePaola anthology. This version contains the moral, "Slow and steady wins the race." Provide the definition of a moral and discuss what this particular moral means.

Use your Comparison Chart to compare and contrast this version with the Castle version.

Enlarge the hare and tortoise patterns on colored tagboard (pages 119 - 120). Laminate the shapes and use a washable marker to make them reuseable.

Reproduce the "The Tortoise and the Hare Cheer" (page 114) on a large sheet of chart paper or on an overhead transparency. After reading it several times to the children, ask them to join in on the repetitive lines in each section. Then have the children color, cut and assemble little books of the cheer to practice and take home (see pages 115 - 118).

Day 3: Ask other children to retell the fable in its classic form. Prompt the students, if needed, to encourage the recall of main events.

Read another version today, such as the colorful Wildsmith version. Add information about this version to your Comparison Chart.

Discuss with your students which parts of this fable are fantasy and which parts are real. Emphasize hares, tortoises, foxes, and so on really do exist, but that they do not wear clothing or speak. This distinction between real and make-believe is an important skill to develop.

Gather a variety of books from your school or classroom library about real animals, such as the *See How They Grow* series published by Dorling Kindersley. Include these books at your Science Center. Read several books to your class, making sure you include a book about rabbits. Discuss how real rabbits and turtles are alike and different. A Venn diagram would be a good way to show this information (see below).

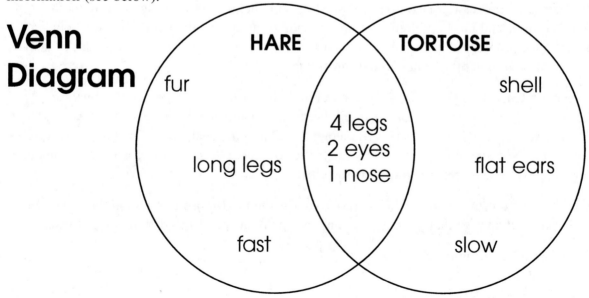

Venn Diagram

HARE   TORTOISE

fur

long legs

4 legs
2 eyes
1 nose

shell

flat ears

fast   slow

Sample Lesson Plans *(cont.)*

Day 3, cont.: As a follow-up to your discussion about real and make-believe animals, reproduce page 122 for each child to complete. Encourage them to use books and posters which you have made available to them as they complete this basic research project.

Reproduce the paper bag puppet patterns on pages 123 - 124 for your students to make their own puppets to use in retelling the fable.

Day 4: Have more children retell the fable, giving prompts as needed.

Read another version of the fable, such as the Stevens version. Add information from this version to both your Comparison Chart and animal list. The Stevens version humorously tells the variety of ways the tortoise works to get in shape before the race. Make a list of things which people need to do to stay in shape and be healthy, including nutritious foods they need to eat. Encourage children to make posters on large sheets of construction paper to advertise the benefits of being healthy and getting in shape. Display the posters in your Science Center.

Extend your students' learning by introducing the Learning Centers for this theme. See page 112 for ideas.

Day 5: Continue to practice retelling the fable.

Make a graph today, letting children vote with their shoes for their favorite version of the fable. First, place a copy of each version on the floor in a straight line. Children put one of their own shoes (athletic shoes would be ideal) in a row under the version of their choice. Then read the class favorite.

As your concluding activity, have a Fitness Festival. Hold your Fitness Festival in a gym or outdoor play area. You may want to dress for the festival in a jogging suit, running shoes, sweatband, and whistle. Begin by discussing the day's goal of becoming physically fit. Remind the children to do their best, though they will not be competing against others. Begin with a warm-up of stretching and bending exercises. Jog in place and then run around the area in "follow-the-leader" fashion a few times. Play a cassette tape with lively music during your warming up and running time.

Next, try calisthenics such as jumping jacks, airplanes, wall pushes, etc. Go on to skipping; hopping; galloping; using hula hoops; jumping rope; and bouncing, throwing, and catching playground balls. Be sure to give your students rest and water times. Return to your classroom to eat the healthy snacks that parents sent in for the festival. Present each child with a Fitness Award Medal (see page 121) and praise each child for effort.

Fitness Award Medal
For _Herbie_
Date _9- 15- 94_

Sample Centers

Reading Center: Keep copies of all of *The Hare and the Tortoise* versions at this center, the group story map made on Day 1, the flannel board shapes, and extra paper bag puppets for children can be used in retelling the fable. The Comparison Chart can be displayed as well for the children to read. Make several extra copies of the "Hare Versus the Tortoise Cheer" and small books for children to practice reading independently or with friends.

Writing Center: Children may write about their favorite sports using a simple writing frame, such as "I like sports. My favorite sport is_____ ." They may then illustrate or cut photographs from magazines to illustrate the sport.

Math Center: Put some colorful shoelaces into your Estimating Jar. As a reference, put ten shoelaces into an identical jar. Compare the amounts in the two jars, and discuss whether estimates should be more, less, or equal to ten.

Reproduce, color, and laminate "The Hare and Tortoise Gameboard" on page 125 - 126 in a file folder. Provide a die for children to use and tell them to practice counting as they move their playing pieces or chips around the gameboard.

Science Center: Display non-fiction books, magazine articles, and posters about real animals at this center for independent study. Your most capable learners may want to look for information about the speeds at which various animals move. Challenge them to find out which is the fastest animal in the world.

Movement Center: If you have a large area suitable for this center, include it during this theme. Encourage children to practice their rope-jumping and hula-hooping at this area. Keep a tape player and cassette of "The Hokey Pokey" here for children to use in small groups.

Art Center: Make a template of a high-top running shoe for children to trace. Children then could trace the shoe shape on a sheet of colored construction paper, adding details with markers, crayons, or scrap materials (lace, rick-rack, yarn, pom-poms, paper scraps, etc.)

Parent Letter

Dear Parents,

Our class is working on a thematic unit based upon the classic fable, *The Hare and the Tortoise.* We will be reading several versions of the fable to compare and contrast, then choosing our favorite version. In addition, we will be learning about real animals and discussing how they differ from make-believe animals.

Throughout this unit, we will be completing writing, math, science, art, movement, and music activities that relate to *The Hare and the Tortoise.* Your child will be bringing home a little book of the cheer, "The Hare Versus the Tortoise Cheer," to read with you. Other learning activities we have planned include:

1. Creating a story map of the main events in the fable.
2. Retelling the story using paper bag puppets.
3. Learning how we can be healthy and stay in shape.

We will conclude our theme with a Fitness Festival on_____, so please remind your child to wear comfortable clothing and shoes to school. We also would like to serve healthy snacks. Please discuss with your child what healthy snacks he or she likes to eat, then plan to send in enough of the healthy snack for your child to share with a few other children. The snacks will be placed on a table in our classroom in "buffet style" for children to sample.

Thank you for helping us celebrate health and fitness!

Sincerely,

(Please return this slip.)

My child will bring _____

as a healthy snack for our Fitness Festival.

Signed _____

 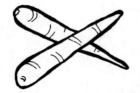 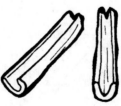 

The Hare Versus The Tortoise Cheer

Hare and Tortoise had a race.
Go! Go!
Slow and steady wins the race.

Hare was fast. Tortoise was slow.
Go! Go!
Slow and steady wins the race.

Hare was running. Tortoise was walking.
Go! Go!
Slow and steady wins the race.

Hare was winning. Tortoise kept walking.
Go! Go!
Slow and steady wins the race.

Hare was sleeping. Tortoise kept walking.
Go! Go!
Slow and steady wins the race.

Hare woke up. Tortoise kept walking.
Go! Go!
Slow and steady wins the race.

Tortoise kept walking and won the race.
Hurray! Hurray!
Slow and steady won the race!

114

Making Little Books

- -

My Little Book of

The Tortoise and the Hare Cheer

Name_____

- -

Hare and Tortoise had a race.
Go! Go!
Slow and steady wins the race.   **1**

- -

Making Little Books *(cont.)*

Hare was fast. Tortoise was slow.
Go! Go!
Slow and steady wins the race.   2

Hare was running. Tortoise was walking.
Go! Go!
Slow and steady wins the race.   3

Making Little Books *(cont.)*

**Hare was winning. Tortoise kept walking.
Go! Go!
Slow and steady wins the race.**   **4**

**Hare was sleeping. Tortoise kept walking.
Go! Go!
Slow and steady wins the race.**   **5**

Making Little Books *(cont.)*

Hare woke up. Tortoise kept walking.
Go! Go!
Slow and steady wins the race.   6

Tortoise kept walking and won the race.
Hurray! Hurray!
Slow and steady won the race!   7

Patterns

Patterns *(cont.)*

Awards

Ticket for
The Hare And The Tortoise Race

I listened to *The Hare and the Tortoise*.

Ask me who won the race.

- -

The Hare and the Tortoise Fitness Award Medal

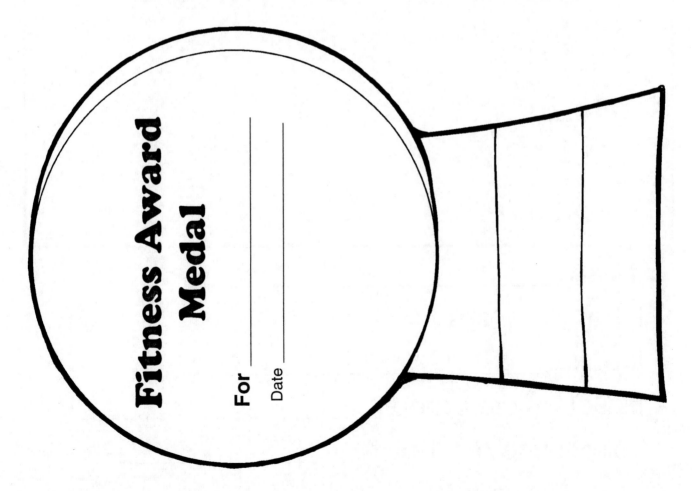

Fitness Award Medal

For _____

Date _____

Researched by _____

Animal Research

This is a real animal.

It is a _____.

[ ]

It lives _____.

It has _____ legs.

It eats _____.

Its babies are called _____.

I also found out that it _____.

Hare Paper Bag Puppet

Directions: Color the hare shapes and cut. Glue the shapes onto a paper bag as shown.

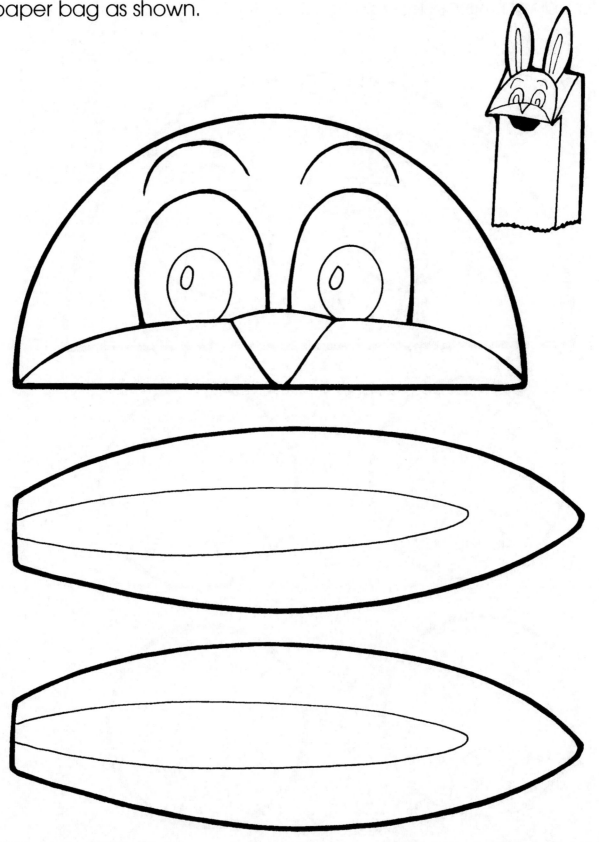

Tortoise Paper Bag Puppet

Directions: Color the tortoise shapes and cut. Glue the shapes onto paper bag as shown.

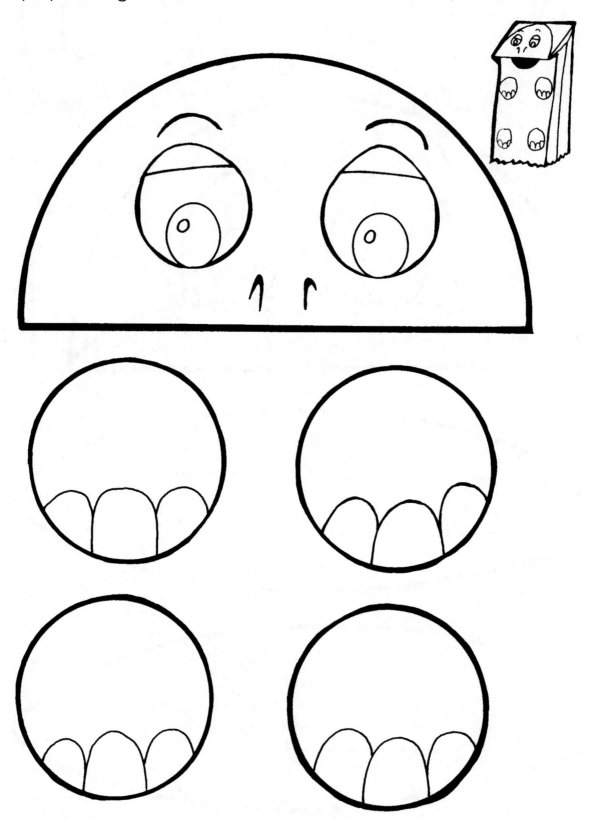

The Hare and the Tortoise Gameboard

Directions: Take turns tossing the die and moving your markers the number of spaces rolled. The first player to reach the Finish Line is the winner.

Taking a nap—lose one turn.

The Hare and Tortoise Gameboard *(cont.)*

Rock slide—
take another
turn.

GO!

Finish

Sample Lesson Plans

Featured Literature: *The Mitten*

Adapted and illustrated by: Jan Brett

Publisher: G.P. Putnam's Sons

Summary: This retelling of an Ukranian folktale is brought to life with the beautiful and intricate illustrations of Jan Brett. A little boy named Nicki drops his new mitten in the snow and it becomes a home for a procession of animals. The mitten stretches and stretches as the animals crowd inside, until a tiny brown mouse squeezes in, bringing the story to an end.

Additional Literature: *The Mitten* by Alvin Tresselt (Lothrop, Lee & Shepard Co., Inc., 1964); *Three Little Kittens* by Paul Galdone (Clarion Books, 1986); *One Snowy Night* by Nick Butterworth (Little, Brown and Co., 1989); *Mouse's Birthday* by Jane Yolen (G.P. Putnam's Sons, 1993).

Related Songs: "Three Little Kittens" from *Mainly Mother Goose* by Sharon, Lois, and Bram (Elephant Records, 1984).

Day 1: Create interest in this new unit by making a display of Jan Brett's books in the reading area. Share a few pages from each book, helping the children notice the unusual illustrations that show some of the story action shown in the borders around the main drawing. Then, if you can, display some colorful mittens nearby on a clothesline or on a bulletin board and challenge the children to find the matching pairs.

Tell the children you will be reading a traditional Ukranian folktale, *The Mitten*. Talk about the Ukraine and locate the area where this folktale originates on a map or globe. Look at a few of the illustrations before reading the book and ask the children what they notice about the character's clothing and the setting of the story. As the story is read, try to get children to predict what animal will find the mitten next. Be sure to discuss each animal as some may be unfamiliar to the class.

Reproduce the poem "Mittens" (page 131) on a large sheet of chart paper or on an overhead transparency and practice reading it with the children.

End today's session by using an assortment of mittens to practice sorting and classifying skills. Sort the mittens by as many characteristics as possible, including size, color, etc.

Send home the Parent Letter found on page 130 .

Day 2: Begin by having the children raise the hand with which they write. Then give each child a sheet of construction paper and have them trace the opposite hand with the fingers together to create a mitten shape. Have children cut out the shape and decorate it. The paper mittens can be placed on a long sheet of paper divided into two columns labeled "left" and "right." Use this display as a graph to show if there are more right-handed or left-handed students in the class.

Sample Lesson Plans *(cont.)*

Day 2, *cont.:* Read the Tresselt version of *The Mitten* and compare it to the story by Brett. Compare many different aspects, including the characters, what the mitten looks like, and the story ending. Discuss how the size of the animals increases until the very last character, which is the smallest.

Talk about what materials are used to make mittens and show some mittens or gloves made of different materials such as leather and wool. Discuss what animals give us these materials.

Day 3: Reproduce the little book of the poem "Mittens" for each student (pages 132 - 135) to color, cut, and assemble the books. Practice the poem many times and send the little books home with the children at the end of the week to share.

Introduce the Mother Goose rhyme of "The Three Little Kittens," which should be familiar to most children, and read the version by Galdone.

Invite a parent or guest speaker to come to the class to demonstrate how to crochet or knit mittens. Show other items such as scarves and sweaters made by the same process.

Play some games in the gym or outside to reinforce the concept of left and right such as "Here We Go Looby Loo" and "Simon Says." Or try a winter relay in which children put on items of winter clothing in order such as mittens, a scarf, and boots. The children run to the finish line, then remove the items as they run back to their teams. If you live in an area that does not experience a winter season, substitute other clothing items.

Day 4: Prepare flannel board shapes from the patterns on pages 136 to 140 and use them to have the children help you to retell the story. (Be sure to cut out two patterns from page 136 so that you can sew or glue together a mitten. Place the animals into the mitten in sequence with the story.) After group practice, choose individual students to retell the story independently.

Brainstorm a list of winter words for later use in the Writing Center. Read some other cumulative stories such as *One Snowy Night* and *Mouse's Birthday*. Have the children complete the mitten matching activity found on page 142.

Extend the childrens' learning of this theme by introducing Learning Centers (page 129).

Day 5: Culminate the week of mitten activities by planning some performances of the Mitten Matinee Theater (see the Dramatic Play Center activities on page 129). Groups of four to five children can perform some of the class' favorite tales such as *The Three Bears* or *The Three Billy Goats Gruff.* An invitation for your show is provided on page 143.

Sample Centers

Reading Center: Put copies of all versions of *The Mitten* at this center. Have the flannel board characters here as an aid for retelling the story. Also have available copies of the little books, the poem printed on chart paper or on an overhead transparency, and sentence strips of the poem for a pocket chart.

Many different matching games can be prepared using laminated mitten shapes and a clothesline. Some possibilities for games are: matching capital and lowercase letters, matching colors and color words, matching initial sounds and pictures, and stringing alphabet letters in order.

Writing Center: Display the list of winter words made on Day 4, listing each word on a colorful mitten shape. The children may make individual mitten shaped books, copying and illustrating five winter words, or you may have each child contribute a page for a class "Big Book of Winter Words." A cover for a class book is provided on page 141.

Math Center: Introduce the concept of finding area. Make some tagboard mitten shapes in various sizes. Provide graph paper with large squares and have the children estimate how many squares it will take to fill the mitten shape. Then have them trace the mitten shape on the graph paper and carefully count the number of squares to discover the area. Counting will be easier for young children if they mark each square as they count.

Place many different colors of yarn wound into small balls or bright spools of thread into the Estimating Jar. In addition to estimating the total number of objects, ask the students to guess which color yarn or thread there is most of in the jar.

Art Center: Have the children create mitten puppets using the materials sent in by parents (lace, yarn, trim, scraps of material, feathers, sequins, buttons, etc.). If you are planning a performance, make characters to go with some of your favorite tales, such as *The Three Bears*. Have some parent volunteers help a few children at a time to complete their puppets.

Science Center: Explore the sense of touch by gathering materials with a variety of textures and hiding them in a box with a hole cut in its side. Children reach into the box to feel the objects with and without wearing mittens, discovering how important their sense of touch is for gaining information.

Dramatic Play Center: Set up your "Mitten Matinee Theater" in this area. Children may use their mitten puppets to act out favorite stories or they can invent their own plays. If you don't have a puppet stage, one can easily be made out of a decorated box.

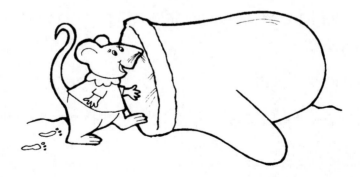

Parent Letter

Dear Parents,

Our new literature unit features a version of the Ukranian folktale *The Mitten* by Jan Brett. We will be reading another version of this tale by Alvin Tresselt and comparing the two stories. During this unit, we will be talking about winter weather and about the concept of right and left. We will also learn the classic rhyme, "The Three Little Kittens."

As a part of this unit, your child will be bringing home a little book to share and read with you. Some of the other activities we have planned include:

1. Making a picture graph about the hand with which we write.
2. Practicing sorting and classifying skills with real mittens.
3. Making a mitten shaped book about winter.

We are planning to set up a special puppet theater called "The Mitten Matinee" where we will perform some simple plays. Our class will be making mitten puppets to use in this center. If you can help, please fill out the form below.

Thank you for your help in our mitten project!

Sincerely,

Name _____

Mitten Helpers

Please check all areas that you can help with and return this note to school by _____.

___ 1. I can send in used, laundered mittens or new mittens for the puppets.

___ 2. I can send in buttons, trim, or material for decorations.

___ 3. I can come in to help the children make the puppets.

_____
Parent's Signature

Mittens

Red mittens
Blue mittens
Mittens for cold weather.

Wool mittens
Knit mittens
Fingers all together.

Lost mittens
Found mittens
Mittens in the snow.

Wet mittens
Dry mittens
Hanging in a row.

Green mittens
Orange mittens
Yellow mittens, too.

Furry mittens
Soft mittens
Which ones are for you?

Making Little Books

- -

My Little Book of
Mittens

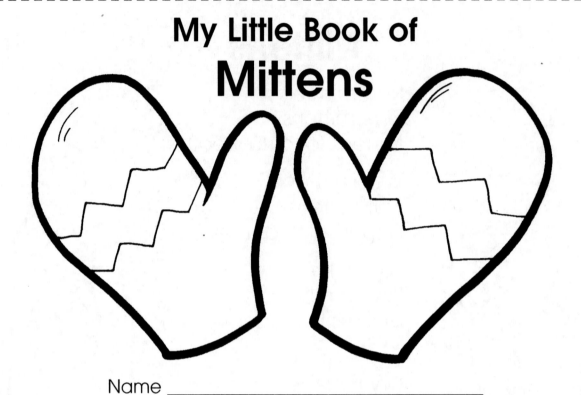

Name _____

- -

Color me
red.

Color me
blue.

**Red mittens
Blue mittens
Mittens for cold weather.**   1

- -

Making Little Books *(cont.)*

Wool mittens
Knit mittens
Fingers all together.   **2**

Lost mittens
Found mittens
Mittens in the snow.   **3**

Making Little Books *(cont.)*

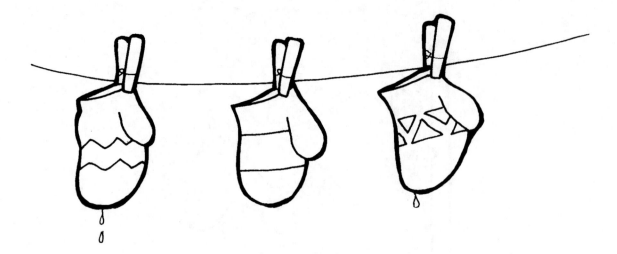

Wet mittens
Dry mittens
Hanging in a row.   **4**

  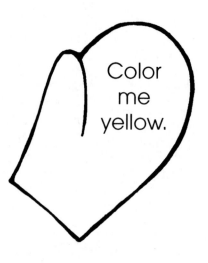

Color me green.

Color me orange.

Color me yellow.

Green mittens
Orange mittens
Yellow mittens, too.   **5**

Making Little Books *(cont.)*

Furry mittens
Soft mittens
Which ones are for you?   6

Mitten Number Page

Directions: Count the mittens by writing in the numbers.

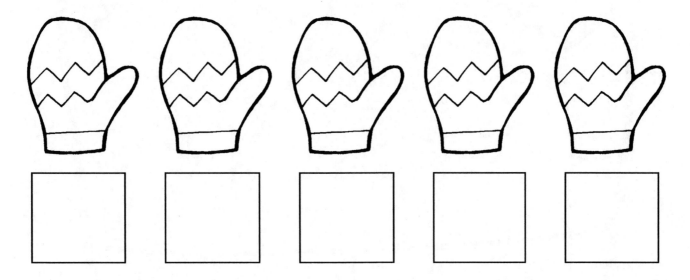

7

Patterns

Teacher's Directions: Cut two patterns, Glue or sew the edges of the mitten, leaving the bottom open. The animals will be placed in the mitten as the story is retold.

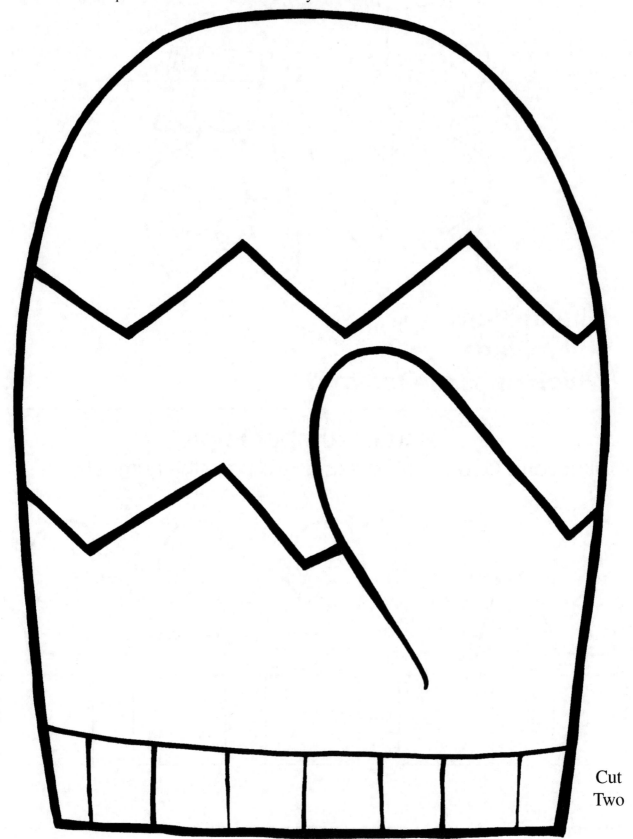

Cut
Two

Patterns *(cont.)*

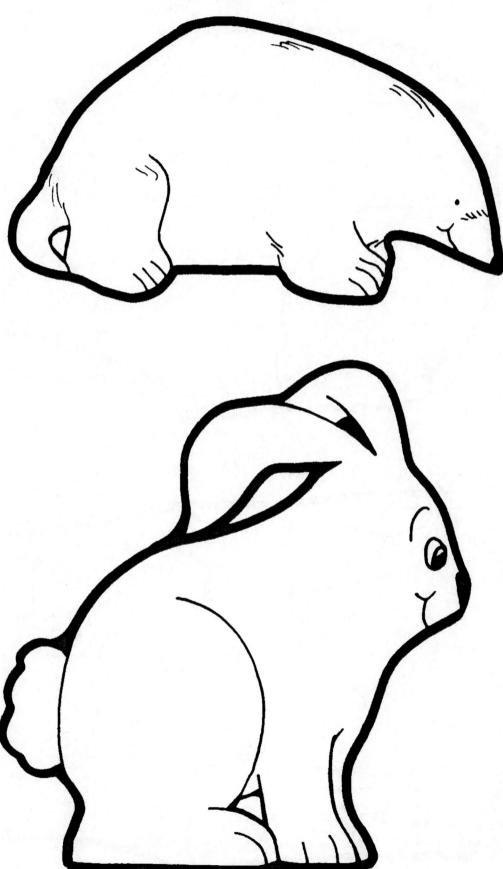

Patterns *(cont.)*

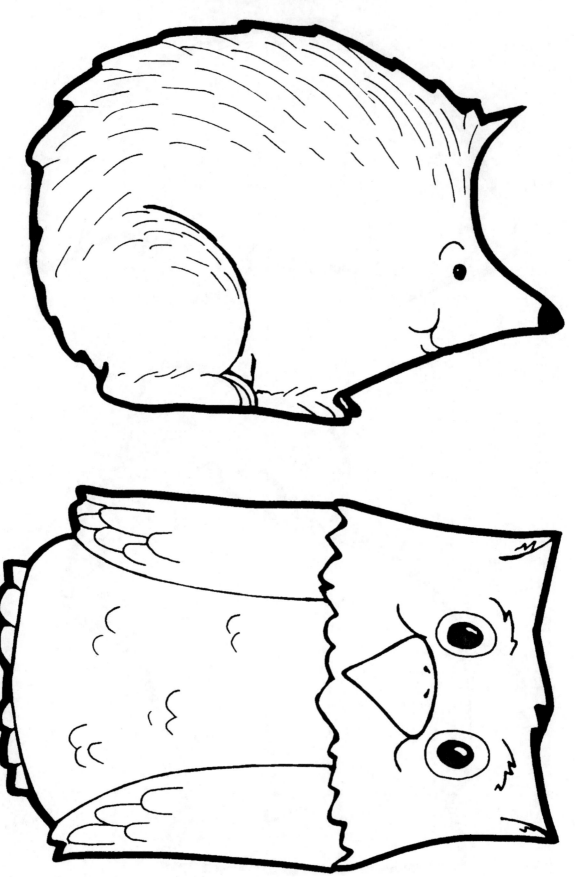

Patterns *(cont.)*

Patterns *(cont.)*

My Book

of

Winter Words

Name_____

Mitten Match

Directions: Cut out the boxes on the dotted lines. Glue each boxed mitten next to a mitten with a matching pattern.

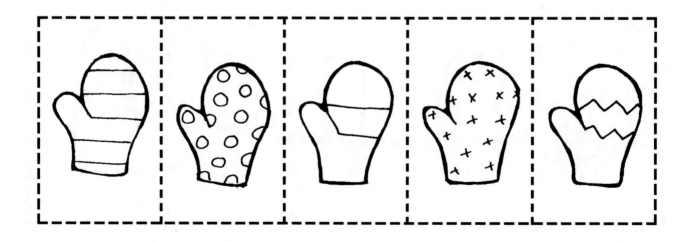

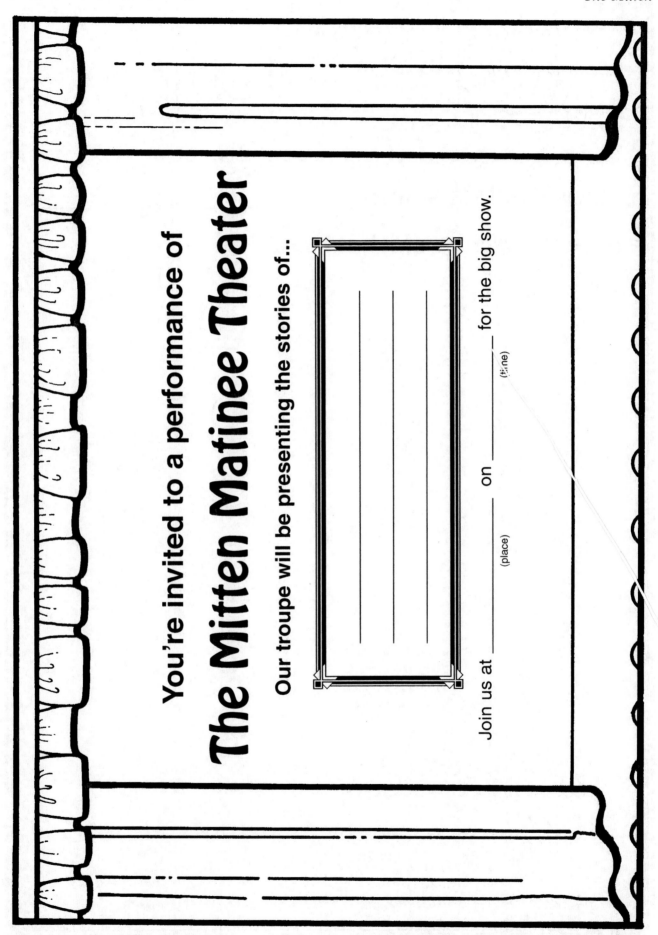

You're invited to a performance of

The Mitten Matinee Theater

Our troupe will be presenting the stories of...

Join us at _____ on _____ _____ for the big show.
(place)   (time)

Junior Scientist's Name:_____

Here is a picture of what I saw.